Jo Parrott

TWO FOR YOUR MONEY

That Patchwork Place®

Credits

Editor-in-Chief: **Barbara Weiland**
Technical Editor: **Laura M. Reinstatler**
Managing Editor: **Greg Sharp**
Copy Editor: **Sharon Rose**
Proofreaders: **Tina Cook, Leslie Phillips**
Design Director: **Judy Petry**
Cover Design: **Darcy Sinclair**
Text Design and Typesetting: **Amy Shayne**
Photography: **Brent Kane**
Illustration and Graphics: **Laurel Strand**

Two for Your Money ©
© 1994 by Iva Jo Parrott
That Patchwork Place, Inc.
PO Box 118, Bothell, WA 98041-0118 USA

Printed in the United States of America
99 98 97 96 95 94   6 5 4 3 2 1

Library of Congress Cataloging-in-Publication Data
Parrott, Jo,
    Two for your money / Jo Parrott.
       p.   cm.
    ISBN 1-56477-073-7 :
    1. Patchwork—Patterns. 2. Machine quilting—Patterns. I. Title.
TT835.P3645 1994
746.46—dc20   94-20459
                                         CIP

Table of Contents

 *Dedication*

To my extra set of hands: Mary Jane Brooks, right hand, and Dana Parrott, left hand. From the inception of this book, through the first strips cut, to the final quilting, they have been there. They only question me once, then if that's the way I want the job done, they do it. I couldn't ask for more. Thank you.

 *Acknowledgments*

My sincere appreciation goes to:

All the pattern testers for checking my math, diagrams, and instructions, and for sharing their ideas and giving encouragement along the way: Audrey Couvillon, Julia Sandlin, Susan Mattox, Linda Alexander, Debbie Duckworth, Mitzi Busby, Leslie Rose, Patti Curtis, Kathy Driskell, Luanne Lee, and Robin Cooper;

My helpers at the shop: Mary Jane Brooks, Dana Parrott, Julia Sandlin, and Lynn Harkins, and Saturday helpers Janet Jelen, Janie Brooks, and Dorothy Burchfield;

My mother, Verniece Snow, for binding all twenty quilts;

Mary Ray for her fine hand quilting;

Henry Parrott, my "other" Saturday and late-night helper, I love you;

That Patchwork Place, Inc., Nancy Martin, and Barbara Weiland and her staff for giving me yet another opportunity to feel good about myself.

Introduction

How Two for Your Money ☐ Got Started ☐

Quilters have always been a frugal group. In pioneer days, fabric was made into clothing and then, when the clothing wore out, the better parts of the garment were saved and included in a quilt. During the Industrial Revolution, scraps from men's shirts were used in quilts. Quilts made during the depression and World War II were made almost entirely from scraps. Only recently have we begun to purchase the entire amount of fabric needed to make a quilt.

Rotary-cutting equipment has made the quilter's life much easier, although even with the new directions and efficient techniques, the quilter accumulates lots of scraps. The scraps from one quilt are usually the same size or shape. In this book, I will show you how, with just a little preparation and planning, you can make these scraps or "cutaways" into another quilt, or maybe into a border for the original quilt. Sometimes, just by adding a few pieces, you can make two different quilts from the same fabrics. Make two gifts at the same time with enough changes that the recipients can't tell you started with the same fabrics!

The techniques used in this book evolved over several years. I found that when I sewed a square to each end of a rectangle to make a large triangle with a smaller triangle at each end, two sets of "cutaway" triangles were made, supposedly to be used "later" in another quilt. As my quilts piled up, so did the stack of cutaway triangles. One day, at a demonstration, I stated that I just never seemed to get back to the cutaway triangles to sew them together and that sewing them was such a hassle. A little voice from the back of the room said, "Why don't you just move over

half an inch and sew the triangles together before you cut, then cut between the two seams?" I stopped, thought a minute, then said, "Good idea!" In another class, a good friend and quilter, Mollie Tabell, when sewing two squares to a rectangle, sewed the wrong direction on the second square. Instead of a triangle, she got a parallelogram. She pondered, "What can I do with these?" I said, "Oh, just about everything!"

So you see, I don't come up with the new ideas, but I do listen to what people say in my classroom. My mathematical mind then starts to calculate squares, rectangles, strips, and yardage. I find this part quite stimulating.

☐ Fast but ☐ Well-Made Quilts

I try to make as many quilts as I can, and to make them as fast as possible without sloppy-looking results. Although traditional patterns are my favorites, I see no reason to apologize for using updated techniques and tools to produce quilts quickly. Properly used, today's tools cut far more accurately than scissors do. A precise $\frac{1}{4}$"-wide seam on a sewing machine can be more accurate than a hand-stitched seam. The introduction of the sewing machine did for seamstresses what the microwave oven has done for cooks. When my grandmother saved her money and bought a machine, she no longer made quilts by hand. We use the best tools we can afford to buy to make our craft and our lives easier.

Machine quilting is finally receiving the acceptance it deserves. Like hand quilting, machine quilting is an art; if you have tried to machine quilt, you can better appreciate fine machine quilting when you see it.

Do the best you can. Practice accurate stitching, but, most of all, keep making quilts. They are a pleasure to make and a joy to receive.

Technique

The technique I use in this book is simple and easy. You won't cut any triangles, only squares and rectangles. The width of the rectangle determines the size of the square. What could be easier?

1. Place the square on one end of the rectangle, right sides together, and draw a diagonal line from corner to corner as shown. Draw a second diagonal line ½" from the first. Stitch on both lines.

2. Cut between the two seams, so the cutaway portion becomes a half-square triangle unit and the rectangular piece has a triangle on one end.

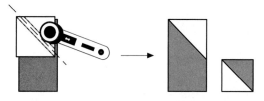

Note: Pressing may distort the cutaways slightly. Just press again to regain their shape. Trim the square if you like, but remember that any additional squares should also be adjusted to the same size.

3. Place a second square on the other end of the rectangle and repeat the procedure for another half-square triangle unit. The original rectangle now has a small triangle on each end and, depending upon how the seam was sewn, has become either a large triangle or a parallelogram. Combine these units to make many different blocks, including all those found in this book.

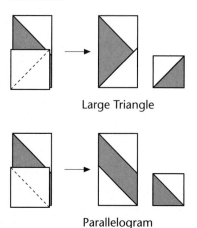

Large Triangle

Parallelogram

When I first researched blocks that could be made without cutting triangles, I sketched 57 different blocks. After you make a couple of quilts using this technique, I hope you will look at blocks in a different light.

☐ Making a Block ☐ the Right Size

All fabric requirements in this book are based on 40" of usable width. All strips are cut across the width of the fabric from selvage to selvage. I calculated the number of crosscuts (second cuts) based on this 40" width, so you may get more squares or rectangles per strip. All cuts include ¼"-wide seam allowances.

Using the Balkan Puzzle block as an example, here's how to calculate the number of squares and rectangles in a block. The block in the example will have a finished measurement of 12" x 12".

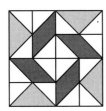

1. Identify the units needed to make the block. Balkan Puzzle is made up of two distinct units.

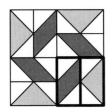

Unit 1   Unit 2

2. Divide the block into a grid of four equal squares across and four equal squares down. To determine each square's size, divide the desired block size by 4. To make a 12" block, divide 12" by 4 to equal 3". (For an 8" block, divide 8" by 4 to equal 2" per square. For a 16" block, divide 16" by 4 to equal 4", and so on.)

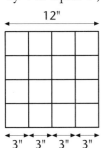

Note: Sometimes a block must be divided into a grid of 5 squares x 5 squares. You must then divide by 5 to obtain the measurements.

3. Unit #1 is composed of 1 square across by 2 squares down or 3" x 6", finished size. Cut the rectangle to measure 3½" x 6½". The two squares added to each end of the rectangle should measure 3½" x 3½".

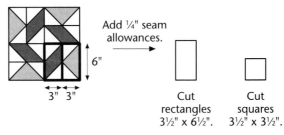

Add ¼" seam allowances.

6"

3" 3"

Cut rectangles 3½" x 6½".

Cut squares 3½" x 3½".

4. The same is true of Unit #2.

5. Compute how many of each shape you need to make a block. (Count how many times each fabric appears in the block and whether it is a square or a rectangle.)

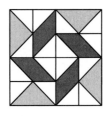

☐ Fabric A: 16 squares, 3½" x 3½"

▨ Fabric B: 4 rectangles, 3½" x 6½"

▨ Fabric C: 4 rectangles, 3½" x 3½"

6. Decide how many blocks to make. A quilt with 42 blocks, set 6 x 7, will measure 72" x 84" without borders. Multiply the total number of squares and rectangles in step 5 above by 42.

> Fabric A: 16 x 42 = 672 squares
> Fabric B: 4 x 42 = 168 rectangles
> Fabric C: 4 x 42 = 168 rectangles

7. Compute the number of strips needed by dividing the width of your fabric (I use 40") by the width of the crosscut to find out how many crosscuts you will get per strip. Then divide the total number of crosscuts by the number of crosscuts per strip.

For example, if we cut Fabric A strips 3½" wide and Fabric B and C strips 6½" wide, and then cut across all strips at 3½" intervals, we will get 3½" squares from Fabric A, and 3½" x 6½" rectangles from Fabrics B and C.

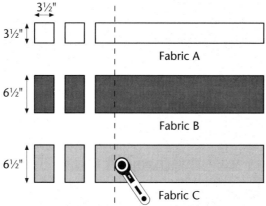

8. Divide 40" by 3½" to get 11 crosscuts per strip. Now divide the total required number of squares (672) and rectangles (168 each fabric) by the number of crosscuts per strip (11).

Fabric A:
Divide 672 squares by 11 = 62 strips

Fabric B:
Divide 168 rectangles by 11 = 16 strips

Fabric C:
Divide 168 rectangles by 11 = 16 strips

9. Convert to yardage by multiplying the width of each strip by the number of strips needed. Divide this total number of inches by 36" to get the yardage amount, then add about ¼ yard for insurance.

Fabric A:
3½" x 62 = 217" ÷ 36" = 6¼ yards

Fabric B:
6½" x 16 = 104" ÷ 36" = 3⅛ yards

Fabric C:
6½" x 16 = 104" ÷ 36" = 3⅛ yards

Use the work sheet on the next page to calculate the fabric you need to make a quilt from the block of your choice.

Work Sheet for Fabric Requirements

1. Name of Block_____ Dimensions_____

2. Grid_____ (4 x 4 or 5 x 5)

3. Unit size_____inches (Divide block size by grid.)

4. Units (Fill in as many as you need; be sure to write each fabric's letter.)

   For example,

5. Number of times the square or rectangle appears in the block (Use more letters if necessary.)
   Fabric A_____ Fabric B_____ Fabric C_____ Fabric D_____ Fabric E_____

6. Cut size of square or rectangle (½" larger than finished size)
   Fabric A_____ Fabric B_____ Fabric C_____ Fabric D_____ Fabric E_____

7. Total number of squares or rectangles needed for quilt
   Fabric A _____ (no. of blocks) x _____(no. of squares or rectangles per block) =_____(total)
   Fabric B _____ x _____ = _____   Fabric C _____ x _____ = _____
   Fabric D _____ x _____ = _____   Fabric E _____ x _____ = _____

8. Use the square measurement from step 6 as the crosscut measurement and divide into 40"
   for the number of cuts per strip. Crosscut measurement_____ Cuts per strip_____

9. Divide the total number of squares or rectangles by the number of cuts per strip to get the
   total number of strips for each fabric.
   Fabric A _____ (no. of squares or rectangles) ÷ _____ (no. of cuts per strip) =_____ (total)
   Fabric B _____ x _____ = _____   Fabric C _____ x _____ = _____
   Fabric D _____ x _____ = _____   Fabric E _____ x _____ = _____

10. Multiply the strip width by the number of strips needed to get the total number of inches
    per fabric.
    Fabric A _____ (strip width) x _____ (no. of strips) = _____ (total inches)
    Fabric B _____ x _____ = _____   Fabric C _____ x _____ = _____
    Fabric D _____ x _____ = _____   Fabric E _____ x _____ = _____

11. Divide inch total by 36" to get the total yardage for each fabric.
    Fabric A _____ (total inches) ÷ 36" = _____ + ¼ yard = _____ (total yards)
    Fabric B _____ (total inches) ÷ 36" = _____ + ¼ yard = _____ (total yards)
    Fabric C _____ (total inches) ÷ 36" = _____ + ¼ yard = _____ (total yards)
    Fabric D _____ (total inches) ÷ 36" = _____ + ¼ yard = _____ (total yards)
    Fabric E _____ (total inches) ÷ 36" = _____ + ¼ yard = _____ (total yards)

Now you know how much fabric to buy, how many strips to cut, and how many crosscuts you
need for the required number of squares and rectangles.

With just a little preparation, you can make any block in this book any size you want and use the
cutaways to make a second quilt. Remember, however, that small squares produce small
cutaways—the second quilt could be a miniature.

Fabric

Choosing fabric should be a happy experience, not the traumatic one some make it. Just relax, think happy thoughts, and choose fabric colors you like. Don't try to precisely match colors from one print to the other. No one can tell if the large flower's small yellow center matches that other yellow fabric used as a square in the outside corner of the block! All you need to know is that they look good together from five to six feet away.

Use 100% cotton fabrics for easier piecing and faster quilting. Prewash all fabrics to prevent shrinkage and bleeding in your finished quilt. If a fabric bleeds, rinse it in cold water until the water runs clear.

Tools

There are many different tools on the market for quilters. I most often use a large-diameter rotary cutter, a 3½" x 23" see-through ruler, and a gridded cutting mat. For special cuts, I use the Bias Square® and a 3½" x 12½" see-through ruler. I prefer a 17" x 23" cutting mat. It is easy to orient vertically, or for crosscuts, horizontally. Never try to use a warped mat, even if just the corner is distorted. It isn't worth it.

A good sewing machine makes everything go together more easily. If your budget allows, treat yourself to a good one. When I purchased my latest machine, I told the dealer all I needed was a good straight stitch and an even-feed foot. Paying for something I wasn't going to use would be a waste. However, even though I didn't need it, the needle-down feature that came with the machine I purchased has turned out to be a joy.

Choose a good iron for pressing. An iron that slides easily on the fabric will help keep the fabric from stretching out of shape.

General Instructions

Read the following instructions before you start a quilt. These instructions are presented up front so they don't have to be repeated with each set of quilt instructions.

□ Cutting □

Unless otherwise stated, cut all strips across the fabric width (crosswise grain). The strips will be approximately 40"–44" long. Fold the fabric lengthwise before cutting, making sure the selvages are even (parallel), and that there are no wrinkles along the folded edge.

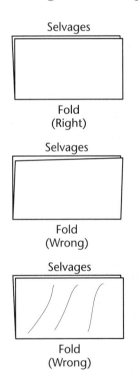

Selvages

Fold
(Right)

Selvages

Fold
(Wrong)

Selvages

Fold
(Wrong)

If your cut looks like this,

it means your fabric was not folded correctly. Even the slightest **V** presents a problem when making the crosscuts. This is why I do not fold fabric a second time. A second fold just gives you the opportunity to get a strip with three zigzags!

1. Lay the fabric on the gridded cutting mat with the fold toward you, the raw edges to the left (reverse if left-handed), and the selvages at the top of the mat.

2. Place the long edge of a ruler along the raw edge of the fabric. To ensure that it is placed at a right angle to the fold, lay one edge of another ruler along the fold and adjust the first ruler so that it is flush with the side of the ruler on the fold.

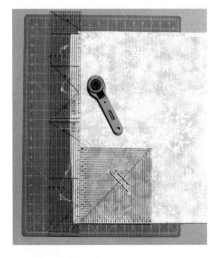

3. Use the measurements on the ruler and mat to keep cuts straight. To cut an accurate 3"-wide strip, place the 3"-line of the ruler on the edge of the fabric. You should not see any fabric to the left of the 3" line, and you should not see any of the mat between the fabric and the 3" line. Remember, if your strips are not cut accurately, there is no amount of sewing that will make your pieces fit.

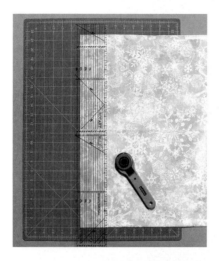

Note: All measurements given for cut strips include ¼"-wide seam allowances. Therefore, a strip cut 3" wide will finish to 2½" wide.

4. After you cut the strips, place them on the cutting mat as shown, aligning one of the long cut edges along a grid line, with the selvage to the left and the fold to the right (reverse if left-handed). Now make your second cuts (crosscuts).

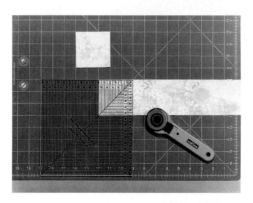

Note: You can stack two strips, then place them side by side with another stack of strips. Stacking three strips will make six layers of fabric, so if you place three strips beside three other strips, you can cut twelve squares or rectangles at a time. This method is accurate and certainly speeds up the cutting procedure.

☐ Pressing ☐

Pressing seams is probably the most neglected technique in quiltmaking. If you press newly cut strips, be sure to press them straight—don't make a canoe out of them.

For rectangle units, sew the square to the rectangle with two seams, cut between the two seams, then press. Press the cutaway squares' seams consistently toward the small triangle. To press the rectangle unit, place the rectangle on the ironing board with the small triangle on top. Lift the triangle and move the side of the iron (not the tip) into the seam. Press the seam toward the small triangle. This method is the easiest and works well in later assembly.

☐ Half-Square Triangle ☐ Units

If you need additional cutaways or make one of the secondary quilts without making the primary quilt, you must make half-square triangle units. Use your favorite method or select one of the following techniques.

Grid Method

For a quick, easy, and accurate way to make half-square triangle units, try this method. For smaller half-square triangle units, I recommend the method on pages 14–15.

1. Place two equal-size fabric pieces with right sides together, light fabric on top. An 18" x 22" piece (fat quarter) works best. Determine the size of the finished half-square triangle unit you need. Add $\frac{7}{8}$" to that measurement. You now know how far apart to draw parallel lines across your fabric. (For example, for a 2" finished square, draw grid lines $2\frac{7}{8}$" apart.) Draw horizontal lines first, keeping lines parallel.

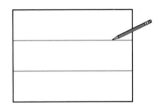

2. Draw vertical lines parallel to each other at exactly 90° to the horizontal lines.

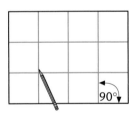

3. Draw diagonal lines through every other square as shown in the diagram. These diagonal lines should go exactly through the corners of the squares.

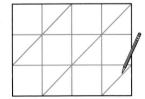

4. Draw diagonal lines in the opposite direction through the remaining empty squares as shown. No square should have an **X** in it. If any do, redraw your grid and diagonal lines.

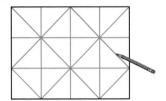

5. Sew a $\frac{1}{4}$" seam on each side of each diagonal line. If you have trouble sewing $\frac{1}{4}$" away, draw a line first. Start in upper left corner and sew a continuous line.

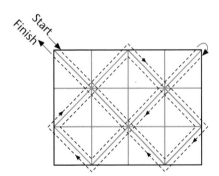

6. After sewing on both sides of all diagonal lines, cut all the vertical and horizontal lines with the rotary cutter, then cut between the two diagonal seams on each square. Press the seam allowances toward the dark fabric.

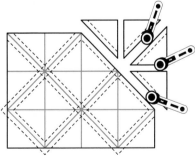

Bias-Strip Method

This method works for all sizes of half-square triangle units, but I especially recommend it for small half-square triangle units (less than 2" finished size). It is the method Mary Hickey prefers and features in her books, including *Angle Antics* (That Patchwork Place).

1. Cut ⅓-yard pieces of two contrasting fabrics and layer them with right sides facing up. Both fabric strips will be cut at the same time.

Layer fabrics right side up.

2. Place the 45°-angle mark of a Bias Square® along the edges of the fabrics as shown, slide a longer ruler against the Bias Square, and make a 45° cut.

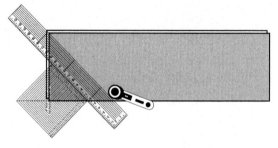

3. Cut bias strips parallel to the first cut. To determine the width of the strips, add ¾" to the finished measurement of the half-square triangle unit. For example, if you need half-square triangle units with a finished measurement of 1¼" x 1¼", cut the bias strips 2" wide (1¼" + ¾" = 2").

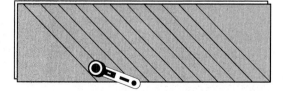

4. Open out the strips and reposition to make units of eight strips each as shown. Stitch together, alternating the fabrics in each unit. Press seam allowances toward the darker color.

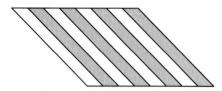

5. Align the 45°-angle mark of the Bias Square along a diagonal seam line. Slide the long ruler against the side of the square and cut away the uneven edges of the unit as shown.

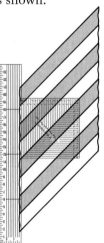

6. Cut strips parallel to the first cut. The strip width should equal the *cut* measurement of the half-square triangle unit. If you need 1¾" x 1¾" cut half-square triangle units, cut the strips 1¾" wide.

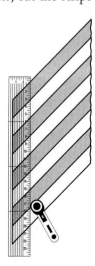

Note: Before you cut each strip, be sure to check the angle of the seam lines, using the technique in step 5 to adjust the angle of the cut if necessary.

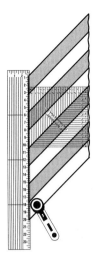

7. Align the 45°-angle mark of the Bias Square along the seam line on the far right, matching lower edges. Cut off the end of the strip at a 90° angle as shown.

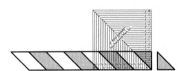

8. Turn the strip around, align the Bias Square's 45° angle along the seam line on the far left, and cut to the desired measurement. Cut remaining squares in the same manner. Trim away any excess fabric to make perfect half-square triangle units.

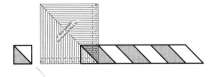

□ Borders □

I do not like to add "busy" borders. Each pattern will give border measurements as I made them. Feel free to improvise and add your own personal touch.

Borders can be mitered or straight-cut. In either case, it is important to measure the finished quilt top carefully to calculate the length of the borders.

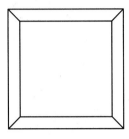

Mitered borders

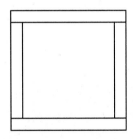

Straight-cut borders

If you purchase enough yardage to cut borders lengthwise, you will not have to piece them. If you cut the border exactly 5" wide, you can get eight lengthwise cuts. This yields borders for both the primary quilt and the secondary quilt. If your fabric is narrower than 40", cut the secondary quilt borders a little narrower.

Look at the other secondary quilts for ideas. You don't have to make the border shown; one alternative is to make pieced borders with cutaway half-square triangle units.

Mitered Borders

For flat mitered corners, follow the directions for the sample quilt below, substituting your quilt's measurements in the formula. The key is accurate measuring and cutting.

1. Measure and record the length and width of the quilt at the centers, from raw edge to raw edge. For the sample quilt below, the width is 52¾" and the length is 74".

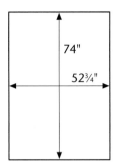

2. Decide on the total finished width of the border(s). I've used a 7" finished width in the example. Add two finished border widths to the measurement determined above.

$$52\frac{3}{4}" \qquad 74"$$
$$+ \; 14" \qquad + \; 14"$$
$$\overline{66\frac{3}{4}"} \qquad \overline{88"}$$

In the example, the top will measure 66¾" x 88" from raw edge to raw edge once borders are added. Cut the border strips ½" wider than the desired finished width, in this case, 7½". Cut two strips, each 7½" x 66¾" (the finished width), and two strips, each 7½" x 88" (the finished length). Be sure these are cut exactly to length.

Note: If you cut the border strips across the fabric width (crosswise grain), it will be necessary to piece them to the correct length(s).

3. At each end of each border strip, measure in and mark the finished border width plus ¼". Mark the center of each border strip.

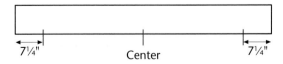

4. Mark the ¼" seam intersection on all four corners of the quilt top. Mark the center of each side of the quilt top.

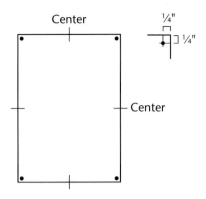

5. Attach all four borders. Match the centers and match the marks at the ends of the border strips to the corner marks on the quilt top. Stitch, easing if necessary. Begin and end stitching exactly at the corner marks, backstitching a few times to secure. Press seam allowances toward the border.

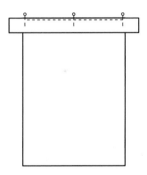

6. With right sides together, fold quilt diagonally so border strips match at one corner. Check to see that the outside corner is square and that there is no extra fullness at the edges. Using a marking pen and a ruler, draw a straight line from the outer corner of the borders to the mark on the border at the quilt corner. Stitch on the line, ending a half stitch from the mark. Backstitch. Trim away excess border, leaving a ¼"-wide seam allowance.

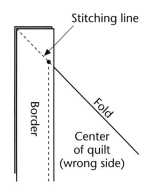

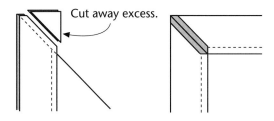

7. Repeat with remaining corners. Press miter seams open.

Straight-Cut Borders

1. Measure the length of the quilt top at the center, from raw edge to raw edge. To determine the cut width, add ½" to the desired finished width. Cut two border strips to that measurement. (For a 7"-wide border, cut strips 7½" wide x the length of the quilt top.)

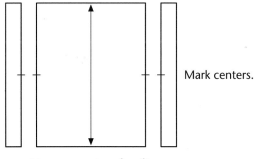

Measure center of quilt, top to bottom.

Note: If you cut the border strips across the fabric width (crosswise grain), it may be necessary to piece the borders to the correct lengths.

2. Mark the center of each side of the quilt and the center of each border strip.

3. Sew border strips to the sides of the quilt with a ¼"-wide seam allowance, matching the ends and centers and easing if necessary. Press seams toward the border.

4. Measure the width of the quilt at the center, from raw edge to raw edge, including the two borders that you just added. Cut two border strips to that measurement in the desired width plus ½" for seam allowances. Mark the center of the top and bottom of the quilt and the center of each border strip.

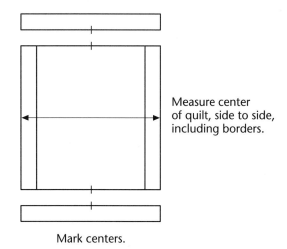

Measure center of quilt, side to side, including borders.

Mark centers.

5. Sew the strips to the top and bottom of the quilt, matching centers and easing if necessary. Press seams toward the border.

▢ Preparing to Quilt ▢

It's easiest to mark the quilt top before layering it with the batting and backing. Choose a marking tool in a color that will be visible on the fabric. For some quilts, you will need more than one color. A mechanical or hard lead pencil is often best for light-colored fabrics. Water-soluble pens are also available, but in my experience, it is sometimes difficult to remove the marks from solid-colored fabrics. You can also use ¼"-wide masking tape as a stitching guide. I recommend positioning it as needed rather than applying it to the entire quilt top, since it may be difficult to remove and often leaves a sticky residue on the surface of your quilt if left in place too long.

To mark dark-colored fabrics, I use a pink or yellow marking pencil, available at your local quilt shop. Both of these show up nicely on nearly all dark fabrics. Whatever you choose for marking, test it first on scraps of your quilt fabric to make sure you can remove it easily.

Once you have marked the quilting design, layer the quilt with batting and backing and baste the layers together.

1. Place the backing wrong side up on a flat surface and smooth it out to remove any wrinkles. Then tape it in place or pin it to the carpet.

2. Spread the batting of your choice on top of the backing, then add the quilt top, smoothing out any wrinkles and pinning through all layers down and across the center of the quilt. Use long straight pins if you are basting for hand quilting. If you prefer, you can pin-baste the layers together for machine quilting, using safety pins spaced a hand's width apart across the surface of the quilt. The thicker the batting, the closer the pins should be.

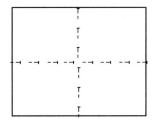

3. Continue pinning, placing pins 3"–4" apart. Using a long darning needle, baste the layers together in a grid, spacing the rows of basting 4"–6" apart. The more you baste, the less likely the quilt layers are to shift while you work.

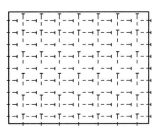

4. Remove the pins and you are ready to quilt. (Leave the safety pins in place for machine quilting, removing them as you go.) The quilting on a quilt is like the icing on a cake. I recommend taking a good class to learn the proper techniques for making the tiny hand stitches every quilter and quilt enthusiast covets.

☐ Binding ☐

To finish the raw edges of your quilt, you will need to make your own binding. Binding can be cut on the straight grain or on the bias. Straight-grain binding requires less fabric, and some quilters say it prevents the outside edge of the quilt from rippling. But because it is cut on the straight grain, there will be a single thread that runs the length of the quilt along the outer edge; it will get more wear than the remaining threads in the binding. That means the edge could wear out sooner. For that reason, I prefer bias binding.

I also prefer double-fold binding for added strength and durability. For this binding, I cut bias strips 2½" wide for a finished width of ⅜".

You will need ½ yard of fabric to make enough double-fold bias binding for a wall or crib quilt. For a twin size, buy ¾ yard. One yard is adequate for either a full- or queen-size quilt, and you'll need 1¼ yards to bind a king-size quilt.

Making Double-Fold Bias Binding

1. Fold a square of fabric on the bias.

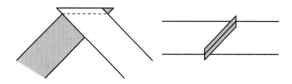

Fold a square on the diagonal.

Bias fold

OR

Fold a ½-yard piece for quick-cutting bias strips, following the illustrations below and paying careful attention to the location of the lettered corners.

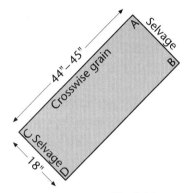

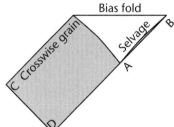

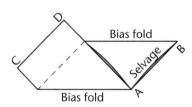

2. Cut strips 2½" wide, cutting perpendicular to the folds as shown.

½ yard of fabric

Bias fold

Square of fabric

3. With right sides together, sew strips end to end to make one long piece of binding. Press seams open.

4. Fold strip in half lengthwise, wrong sides together, and press.

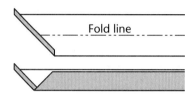

Fold

Attaching the Binding to the Quilt

1. Trim backing and batting so they extend 1" beyond the edges of the quilt top. Trim excess later.

Fold line

2. Unfold the binding at one end; turn under ¼" at a 45° angle as shown to distribute the bulk where the two ends will meet.

3. Start sewing 3" from the turned end. Stitch the binding to the quilt with the raw edges of the binding even with the raw edges of the quilt top. (Backing and batting will extend beyond the edge.) Stitch ⅜" from the raw edges. End stitching ⅜" from corner. Backstitch. Remove from the sewing machine.

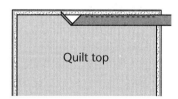

Quilt top

4. To miter the corner, fold binding up, away from the quilt.

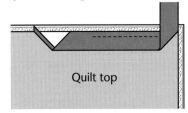

5. Fold binding back down onto itself, parallel with the edge of the quilt. A fold will form in the binding, parallel with the raw edge of the quilt at the upper edge. Start stitching at the edge, ending stitching ⅜" from the next corner. Repeat the mitering steps at each corner.

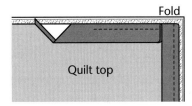

6. When you reach the beginning of the binding, cut binding 1" longer than needed and tuck the end inside the finished edge at the beginning of the strip. Trim away excess batting and backing.

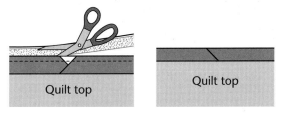

7. Fold the binding over the raw edges of the quilt and blindstitch in place, with the folded edge covering the row of machine stitching. A miter will form at each corner. Hand stitch miters in place.

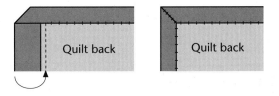

Gallery of Quilts

Hope of Hartford
by Dana Parrott, 1993, Dallas, Texas, 75" x 97". This quilt was originally designed to set square, side by side, but as we started to assemble it, we decided the on-point setting looked better. Pieced by Dana Parrott and hand quilted by Mary Ray.

Flock
by Dana Parrott, 1993, Dallas, Texas, 42" x 42". This quilt takes a little organization to make the different blocks, but the results are well worth the effort. Machine quilted with metallic thread.

Spinning Strips
by Jo Parrott, 1993, Dallas, Texas, 75" x 99". Even with seven different fabrics, the soft pastels of this quilt make it easy on the eyes. Machine quilted.

Amish Bars
by Jo Parrott, 1993, Dallas, Texas, 41" x 53". This secondary quilt makes a great baby gift. Machine quilted by Dana Parrott.

Spinning Strips
*by Julia Sandlin, 1993, Dallas,
Texas, 59" x 84". What a difference
color makes!*

Little Glow Worm
*by Julia Sandlin, 1993, Dallas,
Texas, 40" x 40". Julia chose to take
the cutaway squares from Spinning
Strips and make a different
variation. That's what it's all about!*

Geese in Flight I

by Jo Parrott, 1993, Dallas, Texas, 57" x 89". Plaids are not Jo's favorite, so when her grandson saw this quilt and said, "It's not ugly, it's pretty," it became his. Machine quilted by Mary Jane Brooks, Dana Parrott, and Jo Parrott.

Geese in Flight II

by Jo Parrott, 1993, Dallas, Texas, 64" x 82". This Geese in Flight quilt has a lot more background fabric than the primary quilt. Machine quilted by Mary Jane Brooks and Jo Parrott.

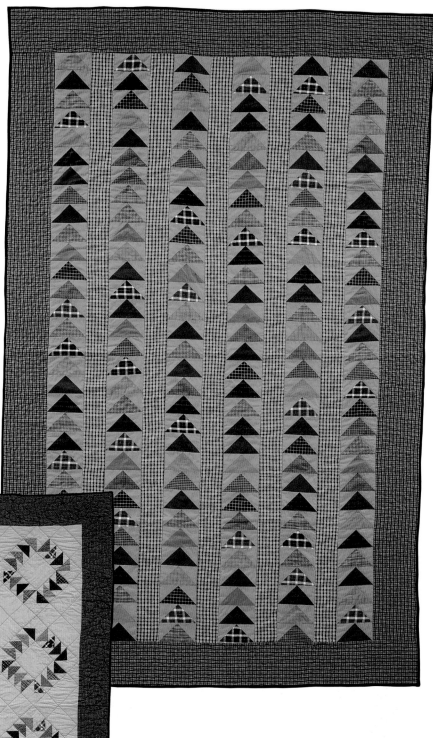

Geese in Flight I
by Audrey Couvillon, 1993, Dallas, Texas, 104" x 104". Keeping the sashing, borders, and background all the same color makes a striking variation.

Geese in Flight II
by Audrey Couvillon, 1993, Dallas, Texas, 67" x 67". Audrey had planned to put the second Geese in Flight on the back of the first quilt but changed her mind and made this lovely wall quilt to hang above the bed.

Clay's Choice
by Jo Parrott, 1993, Dallas, Texas,
70" x 85". This quilt is an old favorite
made with new techniques. Machine
quilted by Julia Sandlin.

Friendship Star with Attic Windows
by Jo Parrott, 1993, Dallas, Texas, 65" x 98". You could
use the cutaways from any of the primary quilt patterns in
this book to make this secondary quilt. Machine quilted by
Mary Jane Brooks, Jo Parrott, and Dana Parrott.

Clay's Choice
(right) by Susan Mattox, 1993,
Dallas, Texas, 84" x 101". Susan used
her cutaway triangles to make a
pieced border for this quilt.

Clay's Choice
by Luanne Lee, 1993, Dallas, Texas,
70" x 85". Luanne chose bold colors to
make this beautiful quilt.

Friendship Star with Attic Windows
(above) by Luanne Lee, 1993, Dallas, Texas, 65" x 98".
The addition of the attic windows makes the secondary
quilt almost as large as the primary quilt.

King's X
by Dana Parrott, 1993, Dallas, Texas, 70" x 85". Here is another easy quilt for the beginner. Pieced by Dana Parrott and machine quilted by Jo Parrott.

Year's Favorite
by Dana Parrott, 1993, Dallas, Texas, 61" x 73". The additional background fabric and the two different blocks make the most of the "cutaway" squares from the first quilt. Pieced by Dana Parrott and machine quilted by Jo Parrott.

King's X
by Kathy Driskell, 1993, Dallas, Texas, 85" x 100". Matching the colors of the border with the on-point pieced squares makes the design appear as a floating grid against a dark background.

Year's Favorite
by Kathy Driskell, 1993, Dallas, Texas, 73" x 85". Cutaway triangles create pinwheels and form larger triangles where the colors are matched.

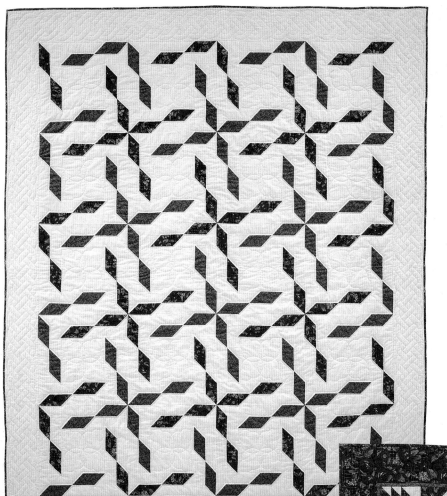

Aerial Spelunker
by Jo Parrott, 1993, Dallas, Texas, 74" x 90". This quilt seemed too pretty for the traditional name, Flying Bats. Hand quilted by Mary Ray.

Indian Trails
by Jo Parrott, 1993, Dallas, Texas, 40" x 50". Here is another stunning way to use those small "cutaways."

Aerial Spelunker
by Debbie Duckworth, 1993, Dallas, Texas, 68" x 86". Debbie added a keyboard border to vary her quilt. Machine quilted by Audrey Couvillon.

Indian Trails (variation)
by Debbie Duckworth, 1993, Dallas, Texas, 62" x 84". Debbie used her cutaways from Aerial Spelunker to make this secondary quilt. Notice the additional fabric on each end of the blocks, making this quilt big enough for a bunk bed. Machine quilted by Audrey Couvillon.

Ribbons
by Jo Parrott, 1993, Dallas, Texas,
72" x 89". The two shades of blue
against the white background make
this a favorite quilt.

Dutchman's Puzzle
by Jo Parrott, 1993, Dallas, Texas, 60" x 72".
Except for the borders, no additional fabric is
needed for this secondary quilt—it makes good
use of the cutaway squares.

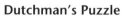

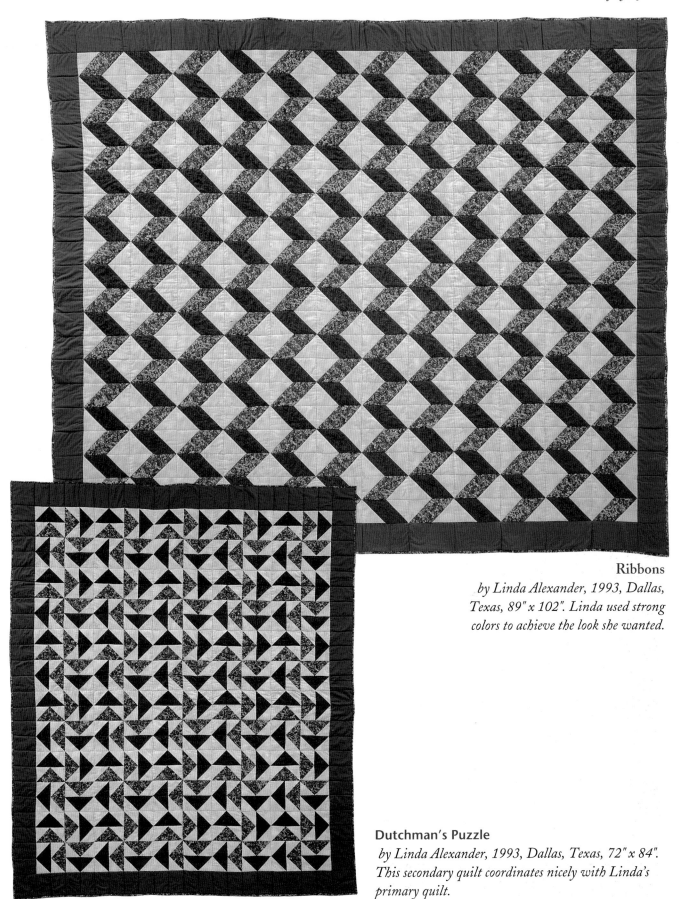

Ribbons
by Linda Alexander, 1993, Dallas, Texas, 89" x 102". Linda used strong colors to achieve the look she wanted.

Dutchman's Puzzle
by Linda Alexander, 1993, Dallas, Texas, 72" x 84". This secondary quilt coordinates nicely with Linda's primary quilt.

Shoo Fly
by Mary Jane Brooks, 1993, Dallas, Texas, 102" x 102". One of the easier quilts in this book, this version would be great for the beginner or the young person just learning to sew. Pieced by Mary Jane Brooks and machine quilted by Jo Parrott.

Four Crowns
by Mary Jane Brooks, 1993, Dallas, Texas, 66" x 102". After making the Shoo Fly quilt, Mary Jane added a third fabric to make this nice-size secondary quilt. Pieced by Mary Jane Brooks and machine quilted by Jo Parrott.

Shoo Fly
by Mitzi Busby, 1993, Dallas, Texas, 74" x 90". Mitzi used only two colors of the cutaway squares to make this dazzling quilt.

Arkansas Traveler
by Jo Parrott, 1993, Dallas, Texas, 85" x 100". This quilt shows a different way to use the easy technique demonstrated in this book.

Hovering Hawks
by Jo Parrott, 1993, Dallas, Texas, 56" x 56". Note the border with the block at the corner—a nice area to show off your quilting.

Arkansas Traveler
by Robin Cooper, 1993, Dallas, Texas, 90" x 106". Robin used cutaway squares in one of the borders in this interesting variation.

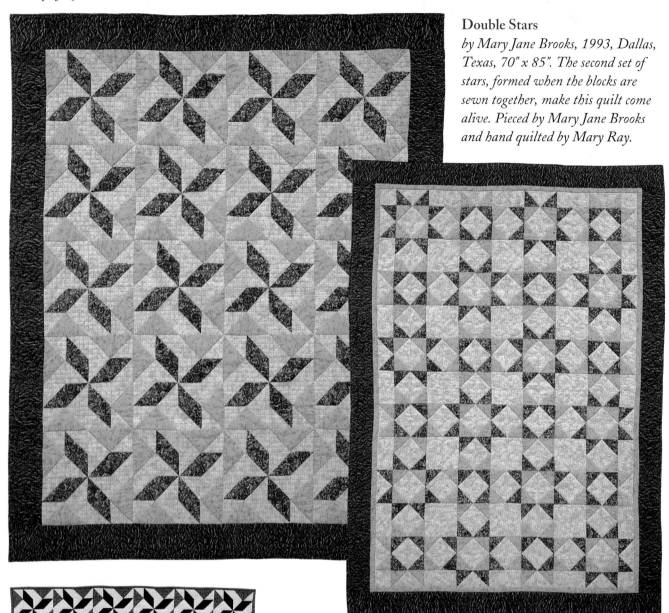

Double Stars

by Mary Jane Brooks, 1993, Dallas, Texas, 70" x 85". The second set of stars, formed when the blocks are sewn together, make this quilt come alive. Pieced by Mary Jane Brooks and hand quilted by Mary Ray.

Variable Star

by Mary Jane Brooks, 1993, Dallas, Texas, 58" x 82". Add squares to the cutaway half-square triangle units, and use two different block combinations to make this second quilt almost as large as the first. Pieced by Mary Jane Brooks and hand quilted by Mary Ray.

Double Stars

by Patti Curtis, 1993, Dallas, Texas, 86" x 86". The contrasting color and value set a strong rhythm, creating the effect of pinwheels flying in the wind.

Variable Star

by Patti Curtis, 1993, Dallas, Texas, 50" x 72". Alternating the placement of cutaway triangles adds interest to this traditional set.

The Quilts

The quilts in this book are presented in pairs: the first, or "primary" quilt, will yield the cutaway half-square triangle units that will be used for the "secondary" quilt. Generally, each secondary quilt will be smaller than its primary quilt. You may enlarge the secondary quilt by choosing patterns with additional half-square triangle units, such as Indian Trails on page 94, or by setting the blocks on point, such as in Geese in Flight II on page 54. The secondary quilts in this book are meant to inspire you and give you ideas for using all the scraps from the primary quilt.

To that end, I have calculated the number of cutaway half-square triangle units that should be left over from each size of primary quilt.

To figure out which size secondary quilt your cutaways will make, compare this number to the number of cutaways from each primary quilt size, which is provided in a separate chart. In general, the smallest primary quilt will yield at least enough cutaways to make the smallest secondary quilt, and so on.

Don't be disappointed if you don't use all your cutaways for the secondary quilt—add them to the border or design a crib quilt for that deserving baby!

For your benefit, I have included fabric requirements for the number of half-square triangle units you will need should you choose to make the secondary quilt without making the primary one.

Spinning Strips

❑ **Block Size: 12"**
❑ **Color photo: page 22**

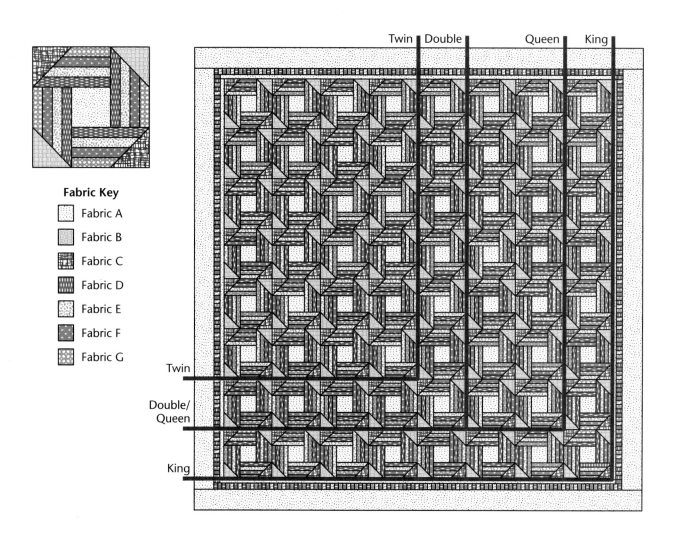

Fabric Key

- Fabric A
- Fabric B
- Fabric C
- Fabric D
- Fabric E
- Fabric F
- Fabric G

	Twin	Double	Queen	King
Size	63" x 87"	75" x 99"	99" x 99"	111" x 111"
No. of Blocks	24	35	49	64
Set	4 x 6	5 x 7	7 x 7	8 x 8

Fabric

Purchase the required yardage for the quilt size you are making.

Fabric Requirements in Yards

	Twin	Double	Queen	King
Fabric A	½	¾	1⅛	1¼
Fabric B	1	1¼	1⅞	2¼
Fabric C	1	1¼	1⅞	2¼
Fabrics D, E, F, G	1¼ ea.	1⅝ ea.	2¼ ea.	3 ea.
Inner Border (crosswise)	½	½	½	⅝
Outer Border (crosswise)	1⅜	1½	1¾	2
OR				
Inner and Outer Borders				
(lengthwise)	2⅝	2⅞	2⅞	3¼
Backing	5¼	6	9	10
Binding	¾	1	1	1¼

Cutting

Cut all strips across the width of the fabric (crosswise grain).
Cut 4½"-wide strips at 4½" intervals to make squares.

	Twin		Double		Queen		King	
	Strips	Squares	Strips	Squares	Strips	Squares	Strips	Squares
Fabric A	3	24	5	35	7	49	8	64
Fabric B	6	48	9	70	13	98	16	128
Fabric C	6	48	9	70	13	98	16	128

	Strip Width	Number of Strips			
		Twin	Double	Queen	King
Fabrics D, E, F, G	1½"	24 ea.	35 ea.	49 ea.	64 ea.
Inner Border	1½"	8	9	10	12
Outer Border	5½"	8	9	10	12

Directions

1. Sew 1½"-wide fabric strips D, E, F, and G together to make strip-pieced units as shown at left. Press all seams in one direction. Use the fabrics in as many different orders as possible.

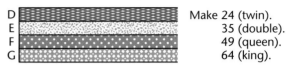

Make 24 (twin).
35 (double).
49 (queen).
64 (king).

Vary the placement of fabric
strips for other units.

2. Cut across each strip-pieced unit to make 4 rectangles, each 4½" x 8½". Reserve the remaining strip-pieced units for the keyboard border. For each block, use a set of 4 rectangles cut from the same strip-pieced unit.

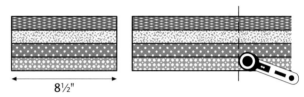

3. For each set of 4 rectangles, sew a square of Fabric B to 2 rectangles, and a square of Fabric C to the other 2 as shown. Sew a diagonal seam, draw a line ½" from the seam, and then sew on this line.

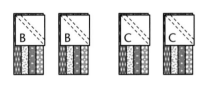

Note: Be sure to sew the diagonal seam from the upper left corner to the lower right corner of each square.

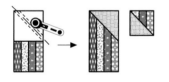

4. Cut between the 2 seams. Press seam allowances toward the triangles. Reserve the cutaway half-square triangle units in sets of 4 for the second quilt.

5. Repeating steps 1–4, cut rectangles from the remaining strip-pieced units and sew to squares B and C in groups of 4 to construct the required number of blocks for your quilt size.

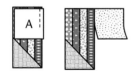

6. Sew a rectangle with a triangle of Fabric B to a square of Fabric A with a half-seam as shown. It will be completed later.

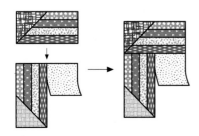

7. Sew the second rectangle with a triangle of Fabric C to the unit made in step 6, as shown.

8. Sew the third rectangle with a triangle of Fabric B to the block as shown.

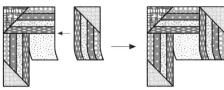

9. Attach the fourth rectangle (with a triangle of Fabric C) to the block as shown. Complete the first half-seam to finish the block.

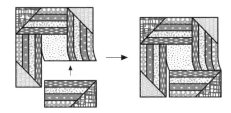

10. Sew blocks in rows, referring to the quilt diagram on page 38. Press seam allowances in opposite directions from row to row. Sew rows together. Press.

11. Cut inner border strips 1½" wide. Refer to the cutting chart for the number of strips for your quilt size. Join strips as needed. Measure, cut, and add side borders as instructed on page 17. Repeat for top and bottom borders.

12. For the keyboard border, cut across the reserved strip-pieced units at 2" intervals to yield 2" x 4½" rectangles.

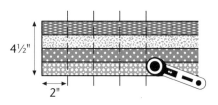

13. Sew rectangles end to end to form the keyboard border, using a random color arrangement.

14. Referring to the border instructions on pages 15–17, measure through the center of the quilt and make adjustments to the border if necessary by resewing some of the pieces, slightly increasing or decreasing seam allowances. A minor adjustment to a few of the rectangles may be all that is needed. Add side keyboard borders, then measure, adjust if necessary, and add top and bottom keyboard borders.

15. For outer border, repeat step 11, cutting strips 5½" wide and joining strips as necessary.

16. Layer backing, batting, and quilt top. Quilt as desired and bind the edges. See the directions on pages 18–20.

two Amish Bars

❑ **Block Size: 6"**
❑ **Color photo: page 22**

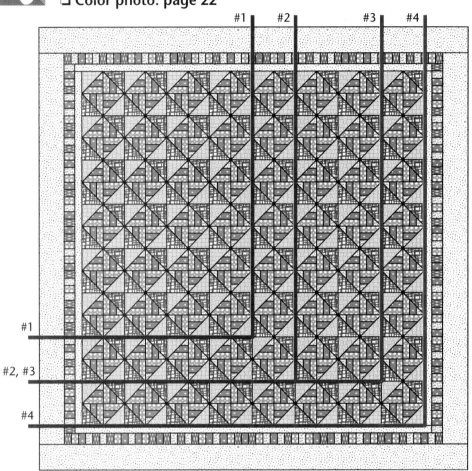

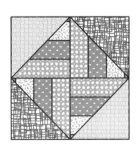

Fabric Key

☐ Fabric A
☐ Fabric B
☒ Fabric C
☒ Fabric D
☒ Fabric E
☒ Fabric F
☒ Fabric G

	#1	#2	#3	#4
Size	36" x 48"	42" x 54"	54" x 54"	60" x 60"
No. of Blocks	24	35	49	64
Set	4 x 6	5 x 7	7 x 7	8 x 8

If you made the Spinning Strips quilt in one of these sizes, you will have the following number of 4½" x 4½" (4" x 4" finished) cutaway half-square triangle units remaining:

	Twin	Double	Queen	King
Fabric A/B	48	70	98	128
Fabric A/C	48	70	98	128

The number of units listed is enough to make the quilt in its corresponding size.

Fabric

Purchase the following additional yardage for the quilt size you are making.

Fabric Requirements in Yards

	#1	#2	#3	#4
Inner Border	1/4	3/8	3/8	3/8
Outer Border	5/8	5/8	3/4	3/4
Binding	1/3	1/3	3/4	3/4
Backing	1 5/8	2 3/4	3 3/8	3 3/4

Cutting

Cut all strips across the width of the fabric (crosswise grain).

Number of Strips

	#1	#2	#3	#4
Inner Border (1½" wide)	5	5	6	6
Outer Border (3½" wide)	5	5	6	6

Directions

1. Using reserved sets of 4 cutaway half-square triangle units from the Spinning Strips quilt, sew squares into blocks. Alternate 2 squares with Fabric B triangles, and 2 squares with Fabric C triangles as shown in the block diagram on page 42. (The strip-pieced triangles in all 4 units per block must be from the same strip-pieced unit.) Refer to the chart on page 42 for the number of blocks for your quilt size.

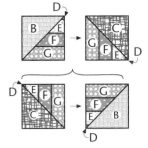

2. Sew blocks into rows, placing Fabric B triangles next to Fabric C triangles. Press seam allowances in opposite directions. Sew rows together. Press.

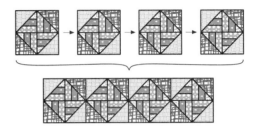

3. Cut inner border strips 1½" wide. Refer to the cutting chart for the number of strips for the quilt size you are making. Join strips as needed. Measure, cut, and add side borders as instructed on page 17. Repeat for top and bottom borders.

4. Make the keyboard border, using the remaining 2½" x 4½" rectangles that you cut for the Spinning Stars keyboard border. Follow the directions in steps 12–14 on page 41.

5. Repeat step 3 above for the outer border, cutting strips 3½" wide.

6. Layer backing, batting, and quilt top. Quilt as desired and bind the edges. See directions on pages 18–20.

 **two** *without* **ONE**

To make Amish Bars without first making Spinning Strips:

Note: The half-square triangle units made below will be slightly larger than the Spinning Strips cutaway half-square triangle units. Each quilt size below will therefore be slightly larger than the Amish Bars secondary quilt made from the cutaway half-square triangle units.

Fabric

In addition to the yardage requirements given in the chart, above left, for the Amish Bars quilt, purchase fabric to make 4⅛" x 4⅛" (3⅝" x 3⅝" finished) half-square triangle units.

Fabric Requirements in Yards

	#1	#2	#3	#4
Fabric B	1/2	3/4	1	1 1/8
Fabric C	1/2	3/4	1	1 1/8
Fabrics D, E, F, G	1/3 ea.	1/2 ea.	2/3 ea.	3/4 ea.

Cutting

Cut all strips across the fabric width (crosswise grain).

	Strip Width	Number of Strips			
Fabric B	4½"	3	5	7	8
Fabric C	4½"	3	5	7	8
Fabrics D, E, F, G	1½"	6 ea.	9 ea.	12 ea.	16 ea.

Directions

1. Sew strips D, E, F, G into strip-pieced units as directed in step 1 of Spinning Stars. Vary the placement of each fabric strip as much as possible.

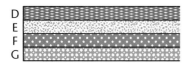

2. Cut across all but 2 (for quilts #1 and #2) or 3 (for quilts #3 and #4) of the strip-pieced units at 4½" intervals to make 4½" squares. Reserve the remaining strip-pieced units to make the keyboard border.

	#1	#2	#3	#4
No. of Squares	48	70	96	128

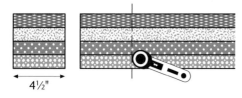

3. Cut across 4½"-wide strips of Fabrics B and C at 4½" intervals to make squares.

	#1	#2	#3	#4
No. of Squares each fabric	24	35	49	64

4. On the back side of the fabric, draw a diagonal line from the upper left corner to the lower right corner of each square of Fabrics B and C. Draw 2 more lines ¼" to each side of the first line as shown.

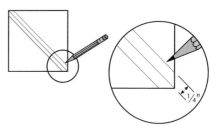

5. Place a square of Fabric B or C on top of a strip-pieced square, right sides together. Stitch along each outer drawn line. Cut along the center line as shown. Press toward the Fabric B or C triangle. Repeat for all squares.

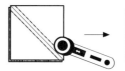

6. Arrange half-square units in groups of 4, alternating 2 squares with Fabric B triangles and 2 squares with Fabric C triangles as shown in the block diagram on page 42. (The strip-pieced triangles in all 4 units per block must be from the same strip-pieced unit.) Sew into blocks. Sew blocks into rows as directed in steps 1 and 2 on page 43. Sew rows together. Press.

7. Measure, cut, and sew 1½"-wide inner border strips to the quilt top. (See step 3 of Amish Bars quilt on page 43.)

8. To make the keyboard border, cut across remaining strip-pieced units at 2" intervals to yield 2" x 4½" rectangles. Join rectangles and add to quilt. (See steps 12–14 of the Spinning Strips quilt on page 41.)

9. Repeat step 7 for outer border, cutting strips 3½" wide. (See step 5 of Amish Bars quilt on page 43.)

10. Layer backing, batting, and quilt top. Quilt as desired and bind the edges. See directions on pages 18–20.

Double Stars

- ❏ **Block Size: 15"**
- ❏ **Color photo: page 36**

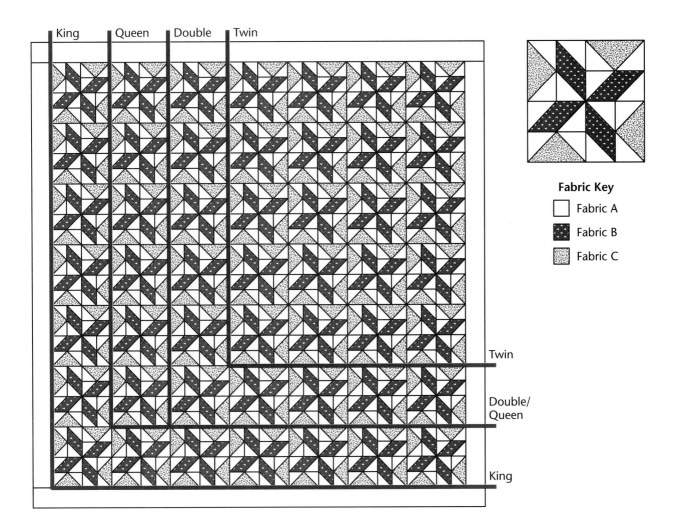

King Queen Double Twin

Twin

Double/
Queen

King

Fabric Key

- ☐ Fabric A
- ▨ Fabric B
- ▨ Fabric C

	Twin	Double	Queen	King
Size	70" x 85"	85" x 100"	100" x 100"	115" x 115"
No. of Blocks	20	30	36	49
Set	4 x 5	5 x 6	6 x 6	7 x 7

Fabric

Purchase the required yardage for the quilt size you are making.

Fabric Requirements in Yards

	Twin	Double	Queen	King
Fabric A	4½	6¾	8	10¾
Fabric B	2½	3⅝	4¼	5¼
Fabric C	2½	3⅝	4¼	5¼
Border (crosswise)	1⅜	1⅔	1¾	2
OR				
Border (lengthwise)	2½	2⅞	2⅞	3⅜
Backing	5¼	7⅝	9	10¼
Binding	½	¾	¾	⅞

Cutting

Cut all strips across the width of the fabric (crosswise grain).
Cut 4¼"-wide strips at 4¼" intervals to make squares:

	Twin		Double		Queen		King	
	Strips	Squares	Strips	Squares	Strips	Squares	Strips	Squares
Fabric A	36	320	54	480	64	576	88	784

Cut 8"-wide strips at 4¼" intervals to make rectangles:

	Strips	Rectangles	Strips	Rectangles	Strips	Rectangles	Strips	Rectangles
Fabric B	9	80	14	120	16	144	22	196
Fabric C	9	80	14	120	16	144	22	196

Directions

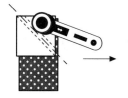

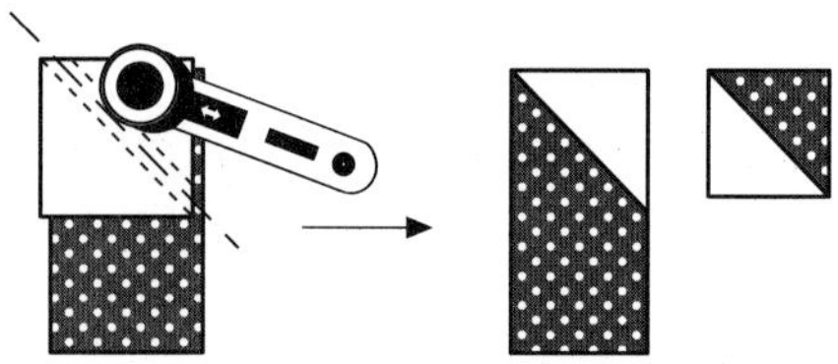

1. Place a 4¼" square of Fabric A on top of a 4¼" x 8" rectangle of Fabric B, right sides together. Sew a diagonal seam from corner to corner as shown, draw a line ½" from the seam, and then sew on this line. Cut between the 2 seams. Press the seam allowances toward Fabric A. Reserve the cutaway half-square triangle unit for the second quilt.

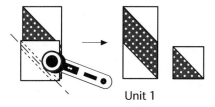

Unit 1

2. Sew a second 4¼" square of Fabric A to the opposite end of the rectangle, with the diagonal seam parallel to the first seam as shown. Sew a second seam ½" from the first, then cut and press as in step 1. Reserve the cutaway half-square triangle unit.

3. Place a 4¼" square of Fabric A on top of a 4¼" x 8" rectangle of Fabric C, right sides together. Sew a diagonal seam, draw a line ½" from the seam, and then sew on this line. Cut and press as in step 1. Reserve the cutaway half-square triangle unit.

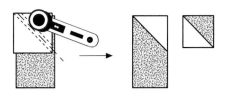

4. Sew a second square of Fabric A to the opposite end of the rectangle, with the diagonal seam perpendicular to the first seam as shown. Sew a second seam ½" from the first, then cut and press as in step 1. Reserve the cutaway half-square triangle unit.

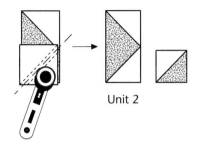

Unit 2

5. Sew each Unit 1 to a Unit 2 to form a pair as shown.

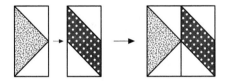

6. Join the first pair to the second pair, rotating the second pair 90° as shown. Repeat with pairs 3 and 4, then join halves to form the block.

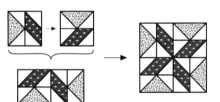

7. Sew the blocks into rows, following the quilt diagram on page 45. Press seam allowances in opposite directions from row to row. Sew rows together. Press.

8. Cut border strips 5½" wide. Refer to the cutting chart below for the number of strips to cut for your quilt size. Join strips as needed. Measure, cut, and add side borders as instructed on page 17. Repeat for top and bottom borders.

5½"-wide Border Strips (cut crosswise)

	Twin	Double	Queen	King
Number of Strips	8	9	10	11

9. Layer backing, batting, and quilt top. Quilt as desired and bind the edges. See directions on pages 18–20.

two Variable Star

❏ **Block Size: 12"**
❏ **Color photo: page 36**

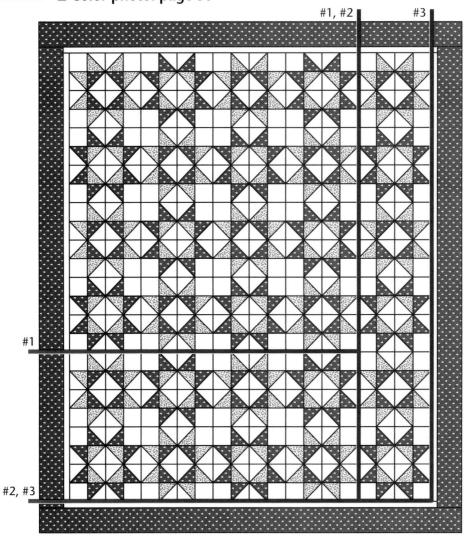

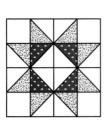

Block A

Block B

Fabric Key

☐	Fabric A
▨	Fabric B
▨	Fabric C

	#1	#2	#3
Size	58" x 58"	58" x 82"	70" x 82"
No. of Blocks	16	24	30
Set	4 x 4	4 x 6	5 x 6

To make Variable Star, you will need the following number of 3½" x 3½" (3" x 3" finished) cutaway half-square triangle units. Refer to the second chart for the number of cutaways remaining from each size of Double Stars. Use extra cutaways for a border or another project.

Total cutaways *needed* for Variable Star

	#1	#2	#3
Fabric A/B	96	144	180
Fabric A/C	96	144	180

Cutaways *remaining* from Double Stars

	Twin	Double	Queen	King
Fabric A/B	160	240	288	392
Fabric A/C	160	240	288	392

Fabric

Purchase additional yardage for the quilt size you are making.

Fabric Requirements in Yards

	#1	#2	#3
Fabric A	¾	1⅛	1¼
Inner Border	⅓	½	½
Outer Border	1	1⅛	1¼
Backing	3⅝	5	5
Binding	½	⅝	⅝

Cutting

Cut 3½"-wide strips across the width of the fabric (crosswise grain). Cut strips at 3½" intervals to make squares.

Fabric A

	#1	#2	#3
Strips	6	9	11
Squares	64	96	120

Directions

1. Arrange half-square triangle units, referring to the block diagrams and carefully noting correct fabric placement. Place a 3½" square of Fabric A at each corner of the block. Sew squares and half-square triangle units into rows. Sew rows together to complete the block.

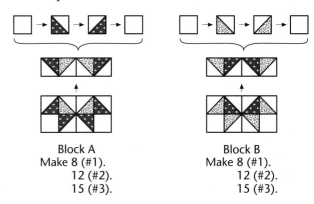

Block A
Make 8 (#1).
12 (#2).
15 (#3).

Block B
Make 8 (#1).
12 (#2).
15 (#3).

Note: To use the most cutaway half-square triangle units, make two different block variations, A and B, as shown in the block diagrams above.

2. Arrange and sew blocks into rows, alternating Blocks A and B as shown in the quilt diagram on page 48. Press seam allowances in opposite directions from row to row. Sew rows together. Press.

3. Cut inner border strips 1½" wide. Refer to the cutting chart below for the number of strips for your quilt size. Join strips as needed. Measure, cut, and add side borders as instructed on page 17. Repeat for top and bottom borders.

4. Repeat step 3 for outer border, cutting strips 4½" wide.

Strip Width	Number of Strips		
	#1	#2	#3
1½"	5	7	7
4½"	6	7	8

5. Layer backing, batting, and quilt top. Quilt as desired and bind the edges. See directions on pages 18–20.

To make Variable Star without first making Double Stars:

In addition to the yardage requirements given in the chart on page 49 for the Variable Star quilt, purchase fabric to make 3½" x 3½" (3" x 3" finished) half-square triangle units.

Fabric Requirements in Yards

	#1	#2	#3
Fabric A	1¾	2	2½
Fabric B	1	1¼	1½
Fabric C	1	1¼	1½
Inner Border	⅓	½	½
Outer Border	1	1⅛	1¼

Directions

1. Referring to the chart for cutaways for the Variable Star quilt on page 49, combine 18" x 22" pieces of Fabrics A and B and 18" x 22" pieces of Fabrics A and C to make the number of 3½" x 3½" half-square triangle units for your quilt size. Use your favorite method or the grid method on page 13. If you use the grid method, draw 4 x 5 grids to make 40 half-square triangle units per grid. Draw the grid squares 3⅞" x 3⅞".

2. Follow the directions given in steps 1–5 of the Variable Star quilt on page 49.

Geese in Flight I

❏ **Block Size: 2½" x 5"**
❏ **Color photo: page 24**

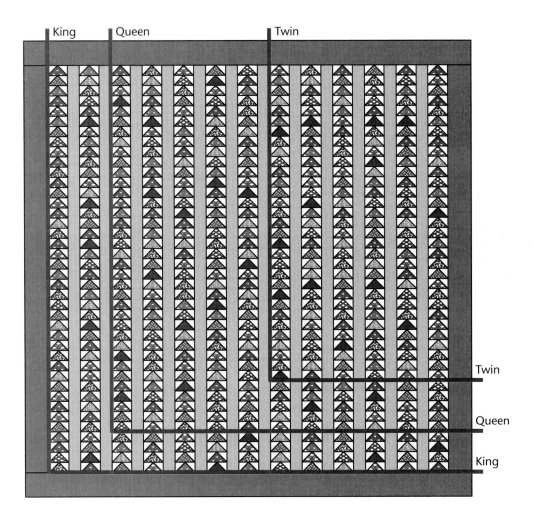

Fabric Key

☐ Fabric A
▨ Fabric B

	Twin	**Queen**	**King**
Size	57½" x 90"	97½" x 102½"	113½" x 112½"
No. of Geese	186	396	520
Set	6 rows of 31 geese each	11 rows of 36 geese each	13 rows of 40 geese each

Fabric

Purchase the required yardage for the quilt size you are making.

Fabric Requirements in Yards

	Twin	Queen	King
Fabric A	2⅝	5⅜	7
Fabric B (or use scraps)*	2½	5	6½
Fabric C (sashing)	2¼	2⅝	3**
Border (crosswise)	1½	2	2¼
OR			
Border (lengthwise)	2⅝	3	3¼
Binding	¾	1	1¼
Backing	5¼	9	9¾

*Illustration shows quilt made with scraps.

**For the king-size sashing strips, all 12 strips can be cut lengthwise only if the fabric is 42" or more wide. If your fabric is less than 42" wide, add ½ yard when purchasing sashing, then cut 1 sashing strip crosswise, piecing as necessary.

Cutting

Cut all strips across the width of the fabric (crosswise grain), except where indicated.

	Strip Width	Number of Strips		
		Twin	Queen	King
Fabric A	3"	29	61	80
Fabric B	5½"	15	31	40
Fabric C	3½"	5*	10*	12*

*Cut lengthwise.

Number of Crosscuts (3" intervals)

	Twin	Queen	King
Fabric A (3" x 3" squares)	372	792	1040
Fabric B (3" x 5½" rectangles)	186	396	520

Directions

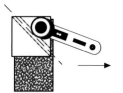

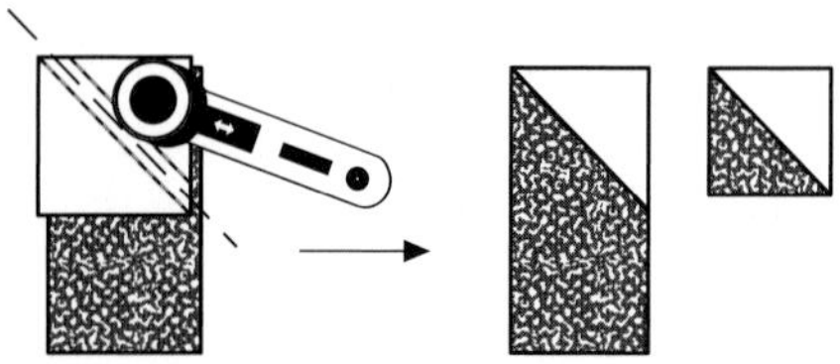

1. Place a 3" square of Fabric A on top of a 3" x 5½" rectangle of Fabric B, right sides together. Sew a diagonal seam on the square from corner to corner. Draw a line ½" from the seam, then sew on this line. Cut between the 2 seams. Press the seam allowances toward the Fabric A triangle. Reserve the cutaway half-square triangle unit for the second quilt.

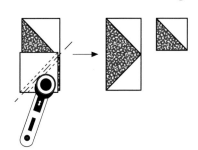

2. Place a second square of Fabric A on the opposite end of the rectangle with right sides together. Sew a diagonal seam perpendicular to the first seam as shown. Sew a second seam ½" from the first; cut between the seams. Press toward Fabric A. Reserve the cutaway half-square triangle unit.

3. Sew Flying Geese blocks into rows for the size quilt you are making. With right sides together, sew along the edge with the point of the triangle, where you can see the X. Sew just a thread's width outside the point where these seams cross.

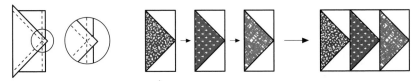

4. Make all geese strips the same length.

5. Cut sashing strips the same length as the geese strips. Cut all sashing strips lengthwise, except the twelfth strip for the King size. Cut that strip crosswise, piecing as needed, and trim to match other sashing strips.

6. After you cut the sashing strips, fold each strip in half to find the center. Repeat with the geese strips. Match the center points; mark or pin. Pin strips together at each end, adjust fullness, and sew.

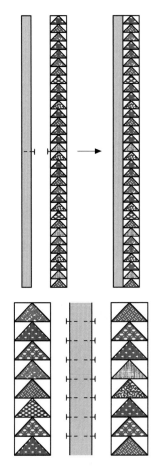

Note: For pinpoint accuracy, mark or pin both edges of sashing strips every 2½". Join to geese rows, aligning seams with marks.

7. Cut border strips 6½" wide. Refer to the cutting chart below for the number of strips to cut for your quilt size. Join strips as needed. Measure, cut, and add side borders as instructed on page 17. Repeat for top and bottom borders.

6½"-wide Border Strips (cut crosswise)

	Twin	Queen	King
Number of Strips	7	10	11

8. Layer backing, batting, and quilt top. Quilt as desired and bind the edges. See directions on pages 18–20.

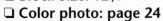Geese in Flight II

❏ **Block Size:** 12¼"
❏ **Color photo: page 24**

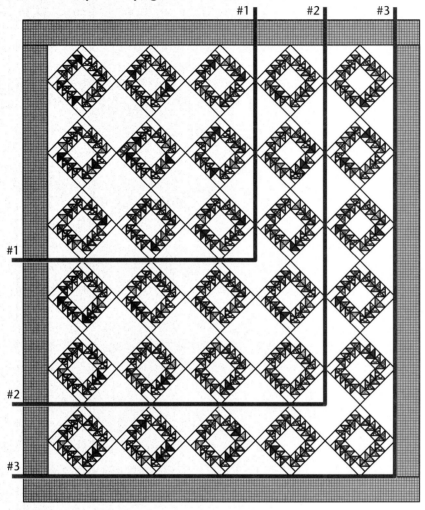

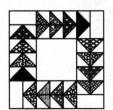

Fabric Key

☐ Fabric A

▨ Fabric B

To make Geese in Flight II, you will need the following number of 2½" x 2½" (1¾" x 1¾" finished) cutaway half-square triangle units. Refer to the second chart for the number of cutaways remaining from each size of Geese in Flight I. Use extra cutaways for a border or another project.

	#1	#2	#3
Size	64" x 64"	82" x 99"	99" x 117"
No. of Blocks	9	20	30
Set	3 x 3	4 x 5	5 x 6

Total cutaways *needed* for Geese in Flight II

#1	#2	#3
288	640	960

Cutaways *remaining* from Geese in Flight I

Twin	Queen	King
372	792	1,040

Fabric

Purchase additional yardage for the quilt size you are making.

Fabric Requirements in Yards

	#1	#2	#3
Fabric A			
(alternate blocks)	2½	3¾	6¾
Border (crosswise)	1½	1⅞	2¼
Or			
Border (lengthwise)	1⅞	3	3½
Backing	4	7⅓	9
Binding	¾	1	1¼

Cutting

Cut all strips across the width of the fabric (crosswise grain).

	First Cut		Second Cut	
	Strip Width	No. of Strips	Dimensions	No. of Pieces
Size #1				
Fabric A	4"	3	2¼" x 4"	36
	5¾"	2	5¾" x 5¾"	9
	9⅝"	1	9⅝" x 9⅝"	2*
	12¾"	2	12¾" x 12¾"	4
	18¾"	1	18¾" x 18¾"	2**
Size #2				
Fabric A	4"	5	2¼" x 4"	80
	5¾"	3	5¾" x 5¾"	20
	9⅝"	1	9⅝" x 9⅝"	2*
	12¾"	3	12¾" x 12¾"	12
	18¾"	2	18¾" x 18¾"	4**
Size #3				
Fabric A	4"	8	2¼" x 4"	120
	5¾"	5	5¾" x 5¾"	30
	9⅝"	1	9⅝" x 9⅝"	2*
	12¾"	7	12¾" x 12¾"	20
	18¾"	3	18¾" x 18¾"	5**

*Cut each square in half once diagonally for 2 corner triangles.

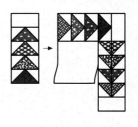

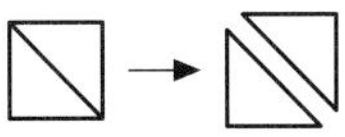

**Cut each square in half twice diagonally for 4 side triangles.

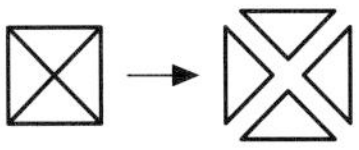

Directions

1. Sew 2 cutaway half-square triangle units together to make each Flying Geese unit, matching Fabric B triangles as shown.

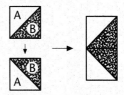

2. Sew 4 Flying Geese units and a 2¼" x 4" Fabric A rectangle to make a 4" x 9¼" Flying Geese strip as shown. Make 4 Flying Geese strips for each block.

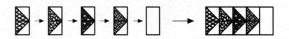

3. Join 1 Flying Geese strip to a 5¾" center square of Fabric A, sewing a half-seam as shown. You will complete it later.

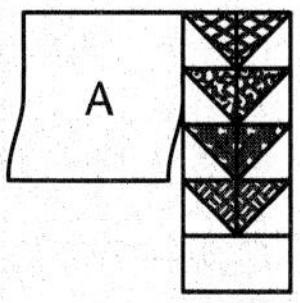

4. Sew a second strip to the center square unit as shown.

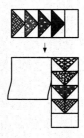

5. Add the remaining 2 strips as shown.

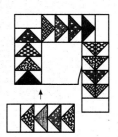

6. Complete the first half-seam to finish the block.

7. Arrange blocks and side triangles into diagonal rows, alternating Geese in Flight blocks with 12¾" squares of Fabric A. Sew blocks and side triangles together, pressing seam allowances in opposite directions from row to row.

8. Sew rows together, adding corner triangles last. Press.

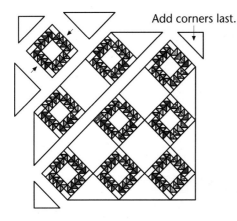

Add corners last.

9. Cut border strips 6½" wide. Refer to the cutting chart below for the number of strips for your quilt size. Join strips as needed. Measure, cut, and add side borders as instructed on page 17. Repeat for top and bottom borders.

6½"-wide Border Strips (cut crosswise)

	#1	#2	#3
Number of Strips	6	9	11

10. Layer backing, batting, and quilt top. Quilt as desired and bind the edges. See directions on pages 18–20.

To make Geese in Flight II without first making Geese in Flight I:

Fabric

In addition to the yardage requirements given in the chart on page 55 for the Geese in Flight II quilt, purchase fabric to make 2¼" x 2¼" (1¾" x 1¾" finished) half-square triangle units.

Fabric Requirements in Yards

	#1	#2	#3
Fabric A	1¼	2	3
Fabric B	1¼	2	3
OR			
10" x 10" scraps	16	36	54

Directions

1. If you have used yardage for Fabric B instead of scrap squares, place Fabric A and Fabric B right sides together. Referring to the chart for cutaways on page 55, construct the number of half-square triangle units required for your quilt size, using your favorite method or the grid method on page 13. If you use the grid method, draw 4 x 5 grids to make 40 half-square triangle units per grid. Draw each grid square 2⅝" x 2⅝".

2. If you are using 10" x 10" scraps for Fabric B, cut the same number of 10" squares from Fabric A.

3. Place a 10" square of Fabric A on a 10" square of Fabric B, right sides together. Construct a 3 x 3 grid for making half-square triangle units. (See step 1 above.) Repeat with the remaining 10" squares of Fabrics A and B to make the number of half-square triangle units required for your quilt size.

4. Assemble blocks, add borders, and finish quilt, following steps 1–10 for the Geese in Flight II quilt on pages 55–56.

Clay's Choice

❏ **Block Size: 15"**
❏ **Color photo: page 27**

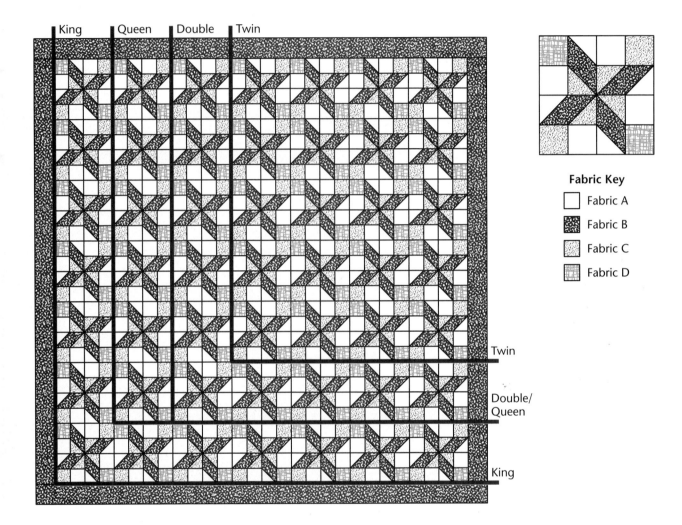

Fabric Key

- ☐ Fabric A
- ▨ Fabric B
- ▨ Fabric C
- ▨ Fabric D

	Twin	Double	Queen	King
Size	70" x 85"	85" x 100"	100" x 100"	115" x 115"
No. of Blocks	20	30	36	49
Set	4 x 5	5 x 6	6 x 6	7 x 7

Fabric

Purchase the required yardage for the quilt size you are making.

Fabric Requirements in Yards

	Twin	Double	Queen	King
Fabric A	2½	3⅝	4⅛	5⅝
Fabric B	2¼	3½	4	5⅜
Fabric C	1⅞	2¾	3⅛	4⅜
Fabric D	¾	1	1⅛	1½
Border (crosswise)	1⅜	1⅝	1⅞	2
OR				
Border (lengthwise)	2½	3	3	3⅜
Binding	¾	1	1	1¼
Backing	5⅜	8	9¼	10½

Cutting

Cut all strips across the width of the fabric (crosswise grain).
Cut only the number of pieces specified; you will use remaining strips to make strip-pieced units.

	First Cut		Second Cut	
	Strip Width	No. of Strips	Dimensions	No. of Pieces
Twin				
Fabric A	4¼"	19	4¼" x 4¼"	80
Fabric B	8"	9	4¼" x 8"	80
Fabric C	4¼"	14	4¼" x 4¼"	80
Fabric D	4¼"	5		
Double				
Fabric A	4¼"	28	4¼" x 4¼"	120
Fabric B	8"	14	4¼" x 8"	120
Fabric C	4¼"	21	4¼" x 4¼"	120
Fabric D	4¼"	7		
Queen				
Fabric A	4¼"	32	4¼" x 4¼"	144
Fabric B	8"	16	4¼" x 8"	144
Fabric C	4¼"	24	4¼" x 4¼"	144
Fabric D	4¼"	8		
King				
Fabric A	4¼"	44	4¼" x 4¼"	196
Fabric B	8"	22	4¼" x 8"	196
Fabric C	4¼"	33	4¼" x 4¼"	196
Fabric D	4¼"	11		

Directions

1. Sew a 4¼"-wide strip of Fabric A to a 4¼"-wide strip of Fabric C to make a strip-pieced unit as shown. Press seam allowances toward Fabric C. Crosscut at 4¼" intervals to make the number of 4¼" x 8" rectangles required for your quilt size. See chart below.

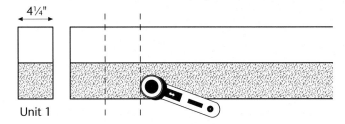

Unit 1

	Twin	Double	Queen	King
No. of Strip-Pieced Units	5	7	8	11
No. of 4¼" x 8" Rectangles	40	60	72	98

2. Sew each remaining 4¼"-wide strip of Fabric A to a 4¼"-wide strip of Fabric D. Press seam allowances toward Fabric D. Referring to the chart above, cut the number of 4¼" x 8" rectangles required for your quilt size.

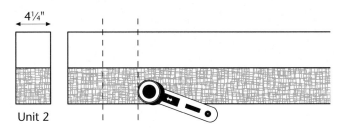

Unit 2

3. Place a 4¼" square of Fabric C on a 4¼" x 8" rectangle of Fabric B, right sides together. Sew a diagonal seam, draw a line ½" from the seam, then sew on this line. Cut between the 2 seams. Press the seam allowances toward the triangle. Reserve the cutaway half-square triangle unit for the second quilt.

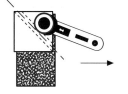

4. Sew a 4¼" square of Fabric A to the opposite end of the rectangle, sewing a diagonal seam parallel to the first seam as shown. Sew a second seam ½" from the first. Cut between the 2 seams and press the seam allowances toward Fabric A. Reserve the cutaway half-square triangle unit.

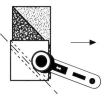

Unit 3

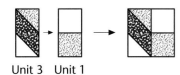

Unit 3   Unit 1

5. Join a Unit 1 to a Unit 3 as shown, matching seams. Press the seam allowances toward Unit 1. Repeat for remaining Unit 1 pieces.

Unit 3   Unit 2

6. Join a Unit 2 to a Unit 3 as shown, matching seams. Press seam allowances toward Unit 2. Repeat for remaining Unit 2 pieces.

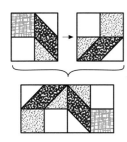

7. Assemble block, using 2 of each unit constructed in steps 5 and 6. Rotate each unit 90°, alternating corner fabrics as shown below.

8. Sew blocks into rows. Press seam allowances in opposite directions from row to row. Sew rows together. Press.

9. Cut border strips 5½" wide. Refer to the cutting chart below for the number of strips for your quilt size. Join strips as needed. Measure, cut, and add side borders as instructed on page 17. Repeat for top and bottom borders.

5½"-wide Border Strips (cut crosswise)

	Twin	Double	Queen	King
Number of Strips	8	9	10	12

10. Layer backing, batting, and quilt top. Quilt as desired and bind the edges. See directions on pages 18–20.

two Friendship Star with Attic Windows

❏ **Block Size: 11"**
❏ **Color photo: page 27**

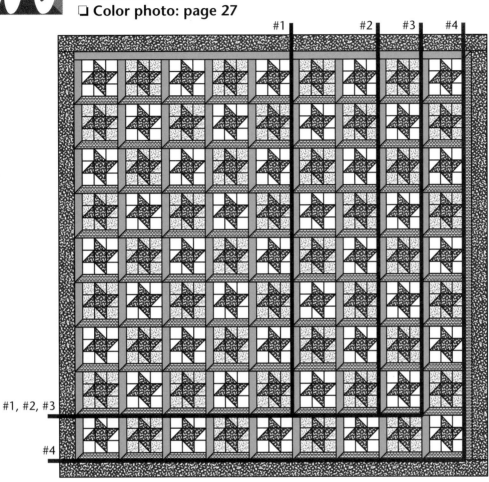

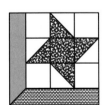

Block 1

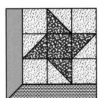

Block 2

Fabric Key

☐	Fabric A
▦	Fabric B
▨	Fabric C
▩	Fabric D
▤	Fabric E

	#1	#2	#3	#4
Size	65" x 98"	87" x 98"	98" x 98"	109" x 109"
No. of Blocks	40	56	64	81
Set	5 x 8	7 x 8	8 x 8	9 x 9

To make Friendship Star with Attic Windows, you will need the following number of 3½" x 3½" (3" x 3" finished) cutaway half-square triangle units. Refer to the second chart for the number of cutaways remaining from each size of Clay's Choice. Use extra cutaways for a border or another project.

Total cutaways *needed* for Friendship Star

	#1	#2	#3	#4
Fabric A/B	80	112	128	164
Fabric B/C	80	112	128	160

Cutaways *remaining* from Clay's Choice

	Twin	Double	Queen	King
Fabric A/B	80	120	144	196
Fabric B/C	80	120	144	196

Fabric

Purchase additional yardage for the quilt size you are making.

Fabric Requirements in Yards

	#1	#2	#3	#4
Fabric A	⅞	1¼	1½	1¾
Fabric B	½	¾	¾	⅞
Fabric C	⅞	1¼	1½	1¾
Fabric D	1⅓	1⅝	1⅝	2⅓
Fabric E	1⅓	1⅝	1⅝	2⅓
Outer Border	1⅛	1⅜	1⅜	1⅝
Binding	¾	1	1	1¼
Backing	6⅛	7⅝	9	10

Cutting

Cut all strips across the width of the fabric (crosswise grain).

	First Cut		Second Cut	
	Strip Width	No. of Strips	Dimensions	No. of Pieces
#1				
Fabric A	3½"	8	3½" x 3½"	80
Fabric B	3½"	4	3½" x 3½"	40
Fabric C	3½"	8	3½" x 3½"	80
Fabric D (blocks)	11½"	3	2½" x 11½"	40
(right inner border)	2½"	3		
Fabric E (blocks)	11½"	3	2½" x 11½"	40
(top inner border)	2½"	2		
#2				
Fabric A	3½"	11	3½" x 3½"	112
Fabric B	3½"	6	3½" x 3½"	56
Fabric C	3½"	11	3½" x 3½"	112
Fabric D (blocks)	11½"	4	2½" x 11½"	56
(right inner border)	2½"	3		
Fabric E (blocks)	11½"	4	2½" x 11½"	56
(top inner border)	2½"	3		

	First Cut		Second Cut	
	Strip Width	No. of Strips	Dimensions	No. of Pieces
#3				
Fabric A	3½"	12	3½" x 3½"	128
Fabric B	3½"	6	3½" x 3½"	64
Fabric C	3½"	12	3½" x 3½"	128
Fabric D (blocks)	11½"	4	2½" x 11½"	64
(right inner border)	2½"	3		
Fabric E (blocks)	11½"	4	2½" x 11½"	64
(top inner border)	2½"	3		
#4				
Fabric A	3½"	15	3½" x 3½"	164
Fabric B	3½"	8	3½" x 3½"	81
Fabric C	3½"	15	3½" x 3½"	160
Fabric D (blocks)	11½"	6	2½" x 11½"	81
(right inner border)	2½"	3		
Fabric E (blocks)	11½"	6	2½" x 11½"	81
(top inner border)	2½"	3		

Directions

1. For each block, select 4 matching cutaway half-square triangle units from Clay's Choice. Each block contains half-square triangle units made from either Fabrics A and B or Fabrics C and B.

2. Arrange half-square triangle units according to the block diagram. Place a 3½" square of Fabric B in the center. For the corners, use 3½" squares of either Fabric A or C, matching the fabric in the block's half-square triangle units as shown. Sew blocks together, referring to the diagrams below.

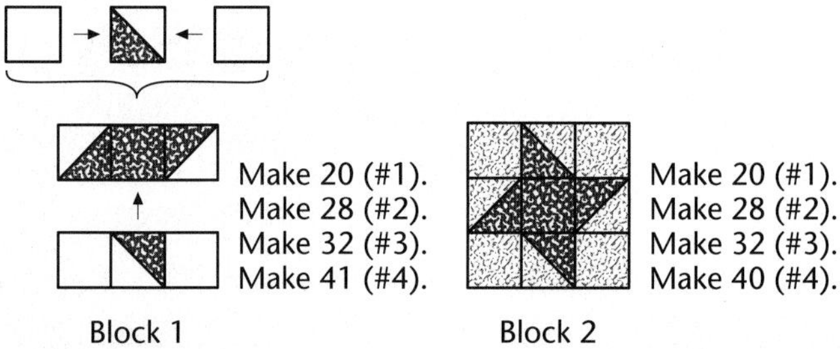

Make 20 (#1).
Make 28 (#2).
Make 32 (#3).
Make 41 (#4).

Block 1

Make 20 (#1).
Make 28 (#2).
Make 32 (#3).
Make 40 (#4).

Block 2

3. To make attic windows, sew a 2½" x 11½" rectangle of Fabric D to one side of each block. Stop ¼" from edge and backstitch.

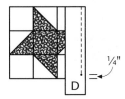

4. Starting at the outside edge, sew a 2½" x 11½" rectangle of Fabric E to the adjacent side of the block. End the seam in the same stitch as the first seam, ¼" from the same corner as in step 3 above. Backstitch.

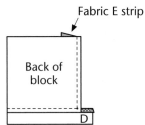

5. Fold the block diagonally so Rectangles D and E match at the corner and face each other, right sides together. Stitch from the outside corner to the point, ending half a stitch away from where the attic window seams meet. Do not catch any of the main block fabric in this seam. Backstitch. Trim miter seam allowances to ¼" wide and press open or toward the dark fabric.

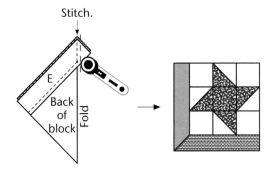

6. Sew blocks in rows, alternating blocks 1 and 2 and keeping Fabric E strips to the left and Fabric D strips on the bottom. Press seam allowances in opposite directions from row to row. Sew rows together. Press.

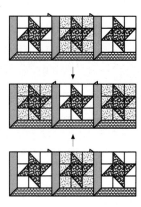

7. From Fabric D, cut the required number of 2½"-wide right inner border strips for your quilt size. (Refer to the cutting chart on page 62.) Join strips as needed. Measure through the center of the quilt from top to bottom and add 2½" for the miter. Cut and sew the border to the right side of the quilt, referring to step 3 and aligning the lower edges.

Note: The lower end of the border is not mitered; cut straight across as you would for a straight-cut border.

8. From Fabric E, cut the required number of 2½"-wide top inner border strips for your quilt size. (Refer to the cutting chart on page 62.) Join strips as needed. Measure through the center of the quilt from side to side, including the border, and add 2½" for the miter. Cut and sew the border to the top of the quilt, referring to step 4 and aligning upper left edges.

Note: The left end of the border is not mitered; cut straight across as you would for a straight-cut border.

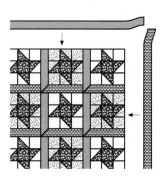

9. Stitch borders together at upper right corner, referring to step 5. Trim seam allowances to ¼" wide and press seam open.

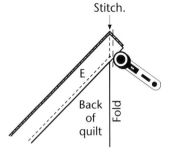

Stitch.

E

Back of quilt

Fold

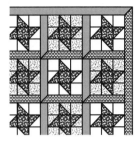

10. Cut outer border strips 4½" wide. Refer to the cutting chart below for the number of strips for your quilt size. Join strips as needed. Measure, cut, and add side borders as instructed on page 17. Repeat for top and bottom borders.

4½"-wide Border Strips (cut crosswise)				
	#1	#2	#3	#4
Number of Strips	8	10	10	11

11. Layer backing, batting, and quilt top. Quilt as desired and bind the edges. See directions on pages 18–20.

To make Friendship Star with Attic Windows without first making Clay's Choice:

Fabric

In addition to the yardage requirements given in the chart on page 62 for the Friendship Star with Attic Windows quilt, purchase fabric to make 3½" x 3½" (3" x 3" finished) half-square triangle units. Refer to the chart on page 61 for the number of required half-square triangle units for your quilt size.

Fabric Requirements in Yards				
	#1	#2	#3	#4
Fabric A	½	1	1	1½
Fabric B	1	1½	2	2⅜
Fabric C	½	1	1	1½

Directions

1. Placing Fabric A with a piece of Fabric B, and Fabric C with a second piece of Fabric B, make the required number of half-square triangle units for your quilt size as shown in the cutaway chart on page 61. Use your favorite method or the grid method on page 13. If you use the grid method, draw a 4 x 5 grid to make 40 half-square triangle units per grid. Draw the grid squares 3⅞" x 3⅞".

2. Assemble blocks, add borders, and finish quilt, following steps 1–11 for the Friendship Star with Attic Windows quilt, starting on page 62.

Shoo Fly

❑ **Block Size: 15"**
❑ **Color photo: page 34**

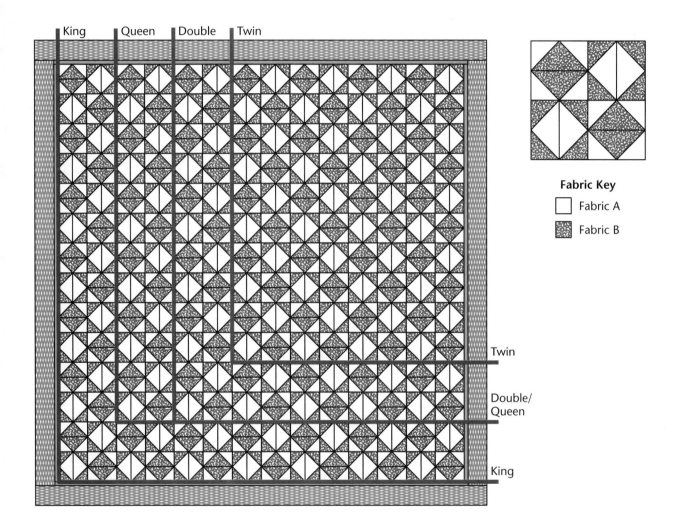

Fabric Key

☐ Fabric A

▨ Fabric B

	Twin	Double	Queen	King
Size	72" x 87"	87" x 102"	102" x 102"	117" x 117"
No. of Blocks	20	30	36	49
Set	4 x 5	5 x 6	6 x 6	7 x 7

Fabric

Purchase the required yardage for the quilt size you are making.

Fabric Requirements in Yards

	Twin	Double	Queen	King
Fabric A	$4\frac{1}{2}$	$6\frac{5}{8}$	$7\frac{3}{4}$	$10\frac{5}{8}$
Fabric B	$4\frac{1}{2}$	$6\frac{5}{8}$	$7\frac{3}{4}$	$10\frac{5}{8}$
Inner Border	$\frac{1}{3}$	$\frac{1}{2}$	$\frac{5}{8}$	$\frac{5}{8}$
Outer Border (crosswise)	$1\frac{3}{8}$	$1\frac{1}{2}$	$1\frac{2}{3}$	2
OR				
Outer border (lengthwise)	$2\frac{1}{2}$	3	3	$3\frac{3}{8}$
Binding	$\frac{3}{4}$	1	$1\frac{1}{4}$	$1\frac{1}{4}$
Backing	$5\frac{1}{4}$	$7\frac{3}{4}$	9	$10\frac{1}{4}$

Cutting

Cut all strips across the width of the fabric (crosswise grain).

	First Cut		Second Cut	
	Strip Width	No. of Strips	Dimensions	No. of Pieces
Twin				
Fabric A	8"	9	$4\frac{1}{4}$" x 8"	80
	$4\frac{1}{4}$"	18	$4\frac{1}{4}$" x $4\frac{1}{4}$"	160
Fabric B	8"	9	$4\frac{1}{4}$" x 8"	80
	$4\frac{1}{4}$"	18	$4\frac{1}{4}$" x $4\frac{1}{4}$"	160
Double				
Fabric A	8"	14	$4\frac{1}{4}$" x 8"	120
	$4\frac{1}{4}$"	27	$4\frac{1}{4}$" x $4\frac{1}{4}$"	240
Fabric B	8"	14	$4\frac{1}{4}$" x 8"	120
	$4\frac{1}{4}$"	27	$4\frac{1}{4}$" x $4\frac{1}{4}$"	240
Queen				
Fabric A	8"	16	$4\frac{1}{4}$" x 8"	144
	$4\frac{1}{4}$"	32	$4\frac{1}{4}$" x $4\frac{1}{4}$"	288
Fabric B	8"	16	$4\frac{1}{4}$" x 8"	144
	$4\frac{1}{4}$"	32	$4\frac{1}{4}$" x $4\frac{1}{4}$"	288
King				
Fabric A	8"	22	$4\frac{1}{4}$" x 8"	196
	$4\frac{1}{4}$"	44	$4\frac{1}{4}$" x $4\frac{1}{4}$"	392
Fabric B	8"	22	$4\frac{1}{4}$" x 8"	196
	$4\frac{1}{4}$"	44	$4\frac{1}{4}$" x $4\frac{1}{4}$"	392

Directions

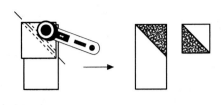

1. Place a 4¼" square of Fabric B on one end of a 4¼" x 8" rectangle of Fabric A, right sides together. Sew a diagonal seam on the square from corner to corner. Draw a line ½" from the seam, then sew on this line. Cut between the 2 seams. Press the seam allowances toward the Fabric B triangle. Reserve the cutaway half-square triangle unit for the second quilt.

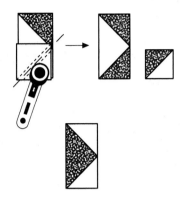

2. Sew a 4¼" square of Fabric B to the opposite end of the rectangle, sewing a diagonal seam perpendicular to the first seam as shown. Sew a second seam ½" from the first as in step 1. Cut between the 2 seams and press as in step 1. Reserve the cutaway half-square triangle unit.

3. Repeat steps 1 and 2, using a rectangle of Fabric B and squares of Fabric A. Press the seam allowances toward Fabric A.

4. Assemble matching pairs to make units, stitching along the long edges of the large triangles as shown.

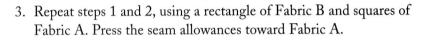

5. For each block, sew 4 units together, alternating light and dark centers and rotating each unit 90° as shown. Assemble the number of blocks required for your quilt size; sew into rows. Press seam allowances in opposite directions from row to row. Sew rows together. Press.

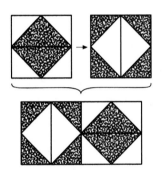

6. Cut inner border strips 1½" wide. Refer to the cutting chart below for the number of strips for your quilt size. Join strips as needed. Measure, cut, and add the side borders as instructed on page 17. Repeat for top and bottom borders.

7. Repeat step 6 for outer border, cutting strips 5½" wide and joining them as needed.

Border Strips (cut crosswise)

Strip Width	Number of Strips			
	Twin	Double	Queen	King
1½	7	9	10	11
5½	8	9	10	12

8. Layer backing, batting, and quilt top. Quilt as desired and bind the edges. See directions on pages 18–20.

Four Crowns

❏ **Block Size:** 18"
❏ **Color photo:** page 34

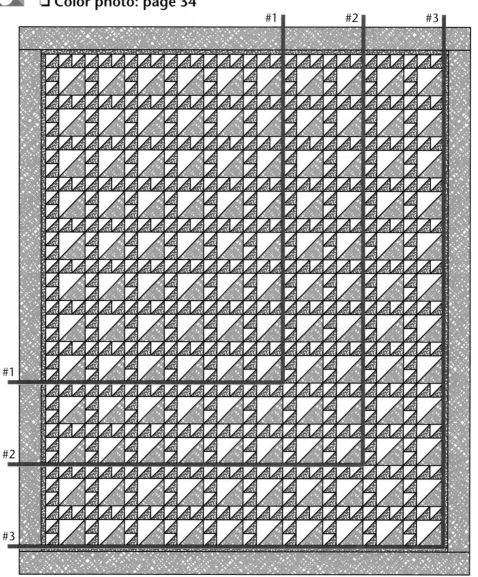

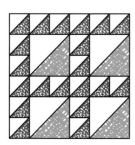

Fabric Key

☐ Fabric A

▨ Fabric B

▨ Fabric C

	#1	#2	#3
Size	66" x 84"	84" x 102"	102" x 120"
No. of Blocks	12	20	30
Set	3 x 4	4 x 5	5 x 6

To make Four Crowns, you will need the following number of 3½" x 3½" (3" x 3" finished) cutaway half-square triangle units. Refer to the second chart for the number of cutaways remaining from each size of Shoo Fly. Use extra cutaways for a border or another project.

Total cutaways *needed* for Four Crowns

	#1	#2	#3
Fabric A/B	240	400	600

Cutaways *remaining* from Shoo Fly

	Twin	Double	Queen	King
Fabric A/B	320	480	576	784

Note: If you made the Queen size Shoo Fly quilt and wish to make Four Crowns in Size #3, you must construct 24 additional half-square triangle units. If you use the grid method on page 13, draw a 3 x 4 grid to make 24 half-square triangle units per grid. Draw grid squares 3⅞" x 3⅞".

Fabric

Purchase additional yardage for the quilt size you are making.

Fabric Requirements in Yards

	#1	#2	#3
Fabric A	1¼	2⅓	2⅞
Fabric C	1¼	2⅓	2⅞
Inner Border	⅓	½	½
Outer Border (crosswise)	1¼	1½	1⅞
OR			
Outer Border (lengthwise)	2½	3	3½
Binding	¾	1	1¼
Backing	5¼	7¾	9½

Directions

1. Referring to the illustration below, make the number of 6½" x 6½" (6" x 6" finished) half-square triangle units from Fabrics A and C for the quilt size you are making. Use your favorite method or the grid method on page 13. If you use the grid method, draw 3 x 4 grids to make 24 half-square triangle units per grid. Draw the grid squares 6⅞" x 6⅞".

Make 48 (#1).
80 (#2).
120 (#3).

2. Sew 2 small (3½" x 3½") half-square triangle units together to make Unit 1 as shown. Sew 3 small half-square triangle units together to make Unit 2.

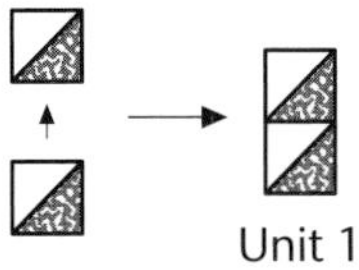

Unit 1

Unit 2

3. Sew a Unit 1 to the left side of each large half-square triangle unit, noting color placement, as shown. Sew a Unit 2 across the top as shown.

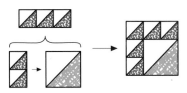

4. Sew together 4 of the units made in step 3 to make each block. Make the number of blocks required for your quilt size.

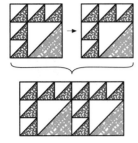

5. Sew blocks into rows. Press seam allowances in opposite directions from row to row. Sew rows together. Press.

6. Cut inner border strips 1½" wide. Refer to the cutting chart below for your quilt size. Join strips as needed. Measure, cut, and add side borders as instructed on page 17. Repeat for top and bottom borders.

Border Strips (cut crosswise)			
Strip Width	No. of Strips		
	#1	#2	#3
1½	7	9	10
5½	7	9	11

7. Repeat step 6 for outer border, cutting strips 5½" wide and joining them as needed.

8. Layer backing, batting, and quilt top. Quilt as desired and bind the edges. See directions on pages 18–20.

To make Four Crowns without first making Shoo Fly:

Fabric

In addition to the yardage requirements given in the chart on page 69 for the Four Crowns quilt, purchase fabric to make small 3½" x 3½" (3" x 3" finished) half-square triangle units.

Fabric Requirements in Yards			
	#1	#2	#3
Fabric A	1¾	3	4⅛
Fabric B	1¾	3	4⅛

Directions

1. Referring to the cutaways chart for the Four Crowns quilt on page 69, make the required number of small half-square triangle units from Fabrics A and B for the quilt size you are making. Use your favorite method or the grid method on page 13. If you use the grid method, draw 3 x 5 grids to make 30 half-square triangle units per grid. Draw grid squares 3⅞" x 3⅞".

2. Assemble the blocks, add the borders, and finish the quilt, following steps 1–8 for the Four Crowns quilt starting on page 69.

ONE Hope of Hartford

❑ **Block Size: 15" (21¼" diagonal)**
❑ **Color photo: page 21**

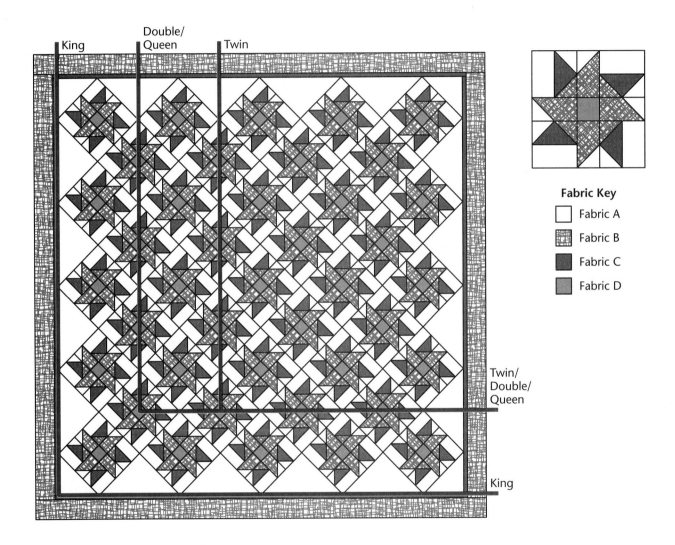

Fabric Key

☐ Fabric A
▦ Fabric B
◼ Fabric C
◼ Fabric D

	Twin	Double/Queen	King
Size	75" x 97"	97" x 97"	118" x 118"
No. of Blocks	18	25	41
Set	3 x 4	4 x 4	5 x 5

Fabric

Purchase the required yardage for the quilt size you are making.

Fabric Requirements in Yards

	Twin	Double/Queen	King
Fabric A	4¾	5⅞	8⅝
Fabric B	2¼	3	4½
Fabric C	1½	2	3
Fabric D	¼	⅜	½
Inner Border	⅜	½	⅝
Outer Border (crosswise)	1½	1⅝	2
OR			
Outer Border (lengthwise)	2⅞	2⅞	3⅜
Binding	¾	1	1¼
Backing	6	8⅝	10⅓

Cutting

Cut all strips across the width of the fabric (crosswise grain).

	First Cut		Second Cut	
	Strip Width	No. of Strips	Dimensions	No. of Pieces
Twin				
Fabric A	6½"	7	3½" x 6½"	72
	3½"	14	3½" x 3½"	144
	22½"	3	22½" x 22½"	3*
	11½"	1	11½" x 11½"	2**
Fabric B	6½"	7	3½" x 6½"	72
	3½"	7	3½" x 3½"	72
Fabric C	6½"	7	3½" x 6½"	72
Fabric D	3½"	2	3½" x 3½"	18
Double/Queen				
Fabric A	6½"	10	3½" x 6½"	100
	3½"	19	3½" x 3½"	200
	22½"	3	22½" x 22½"	3*
	11½"	1	11½" x 11½"	2**
Fabric B	6½"	10	3½" x 6½"	100
	3½"	10	3½" x 3½"	100
Fabric C	6½"	10	3½" x 6½"	100
Fabric D	3½"	3	3½" x 3½"	25

	First Cut		Second Cut	
	Strip Width	No. of Strips	Dimensions	No. of Pieces
King				
Fabric A	6½"	15	3½" x 6½"	164
	3½"	30	3½" x 3½"	328
	22½"	4	22½" x 22½"	4*
	11½"	1	11½"x 11½"	2**
Fabric B	6½"	15	3½"x 6½"	164
	3½"	15	3½" x 3½"	164
Fabric C	6½"	15	3½" x 6½"	164
Fabric D	3½"	4	3½" x 3½"	41

*Cut 22½" squares in half twice diagonally for side setting triangles.

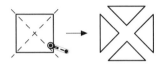

**Cut 11½" squares from remaining 22½" strips. Cut in half once diagonally for corner setting squares.

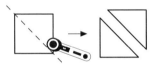

Directions

1. Place a 3½" square of Fabric A on one end of a 3½" x 6½" rectangle of Fabric B, right sides together. Sew a diagonal seam on the square from corner to corner in the direction shown. Draw a line ½" from the seam, then sew on this line. Cut between the 2 seams. Press the seam allowances toward Fabric A. Reserve the cutaway half-square triangle unit for the second quilt. Make 4 of Unit 1 for each block.

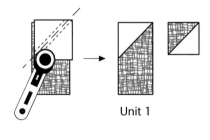

Unit 1

2. Place a 3½" square of Fabric B on one end of a 3½" x 6½" rectangle of Fabric C, right sides together. Sew a diagonal seam on the square from corner to corner in the direction shown. Draw a line ½" from the seam, then sew on this line. Cut between the 2 seams. Press the seam allowances toward Fabric B. Reserve the cutaway half-square triangle unit.

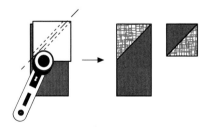

3. Add a 3½" square of Fabric A to the opposite end of the rectangle and sew a diagonal seam perpendicular to the first seam as shown. Sew a second seam, cut, and reserve the cutaway half-square triangle unit. Press the seam allowances toward Fabric A. Make 4 of Unit 2 for each block.

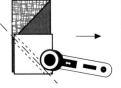

Unit 2

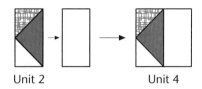

Unit 2   Unit 4

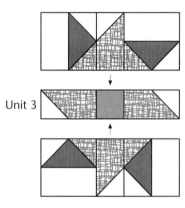

Unit 3

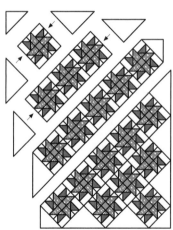

4. Sew the Fabric B ends of 2 of Unit 1 to opposite sides of a 3½" square of Fabric D. Make 1 of Unit 3 for each block.

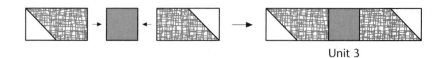

Unit 3

5. Sew a 3½" x 6½" rectangle of Fabric A to each Unit 2 along the long edge of the large triangle as shown.

6. Sew a Unit 4 to each side of a Unit 1, carefully noting the placement shown. Make 2 for each block.

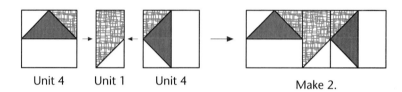

Unit 4   Unit 1   Unit 4   Make 2.

7. Sew a unit from step 6 to each side of a Unit 3 to complete the block as shown. Do not press.

8. Arrange blocks and side triangles in diagonal rows. Sew blocks together into rows, pressing seam allowances in opposite directions from row to row. Sew side setting triangles to the ends of each row.

9. Sew rows together, adding corner triangles last. Press.

10. Cut inner border strips 1½" wide. Refer to the cutting chart below for the number of strips for your quilt size. Join strips as needed. Measure, cut, and add side borders as instructed on page 17. Repeat for top and bottom borders.

11. Repeat step 10 for outer border, cutting strips 5½" wide and joining them as needed.

Border Strips (cut crosswise)

Strip Width	No. of Strips		
	Twin	Double/Queen	King
1½"	8	9	11
5½"	9	10	12

12. Layer backing, batting, and quilt top. Quilt as desired and bind the edges. See directions on pages 18–20.

Flock

❏ **Block Size: 9"**
❏ **Color photo: page 21**

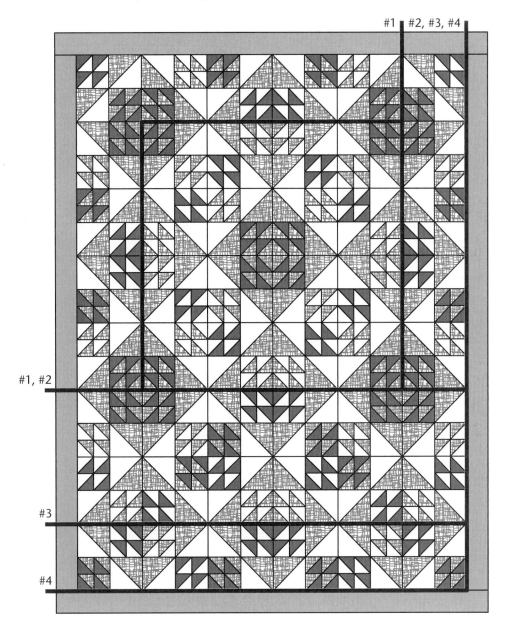

Block 1   **Block 2**   **Block 3**

Fabric Key

☐ Fabric A

▦ Fabric B

▨ Fabric C

	#1	#2	#3	#4
Size	42" x 42"	51" x 60"	60" x 69"	60" x 78"
No. of Blocks	16	30	42	48
Set	4 x 4	5 x 6	6 x 7	6 x 8

Make the number of each block required for your quilt size.

	#1	#2	#3	#4
Block 1	8	8	12	14
Block 2	8	14	18	18
Block 3	0	8	12	16

Note: To use as many of the cutaway half-square triangle units from the Hope of Hartford quilt as possible, use units from two of the three different color combinations in each block. Use remaining units for another quilt project.

To make Flock, you will need the following number of 2¾" x 2¾" (2¼" x 2¼" finished) cutaway half-square triangle units. Refer to the second chart for the number of cutaways remaining from each size of Hope of Hartford. Use extra cutaways for a border or another project.

Total cutaways *needed* for Flock

	#1	#2	#3	#4
Fabric A/B	64	88	120	128
Fabric A/C	32	64	96	120
Fabric B/C	32	88	120	136

Cutaways *remaining* from Hope of Hartford

	Twin	Double/Queen	King
Fabric A/B	72	100	164
Fabric A/C	72	100	164
Fabric B/C	72	100	164

Fabric

Purchase additional fabric for the quilt size you are making.

Fabric Requirements in Yards

	#1	#2	#3	#4
Fabric A	¾	1⅓	1⅓	1⅓
Fabric B	¾	1⅓	1⅓	1⅓
Border (crosswise)	½	¾	⅞	⅞
OR				
Border (lengthwise)	1⅜	1¾	2⅛	2⅜
Binding	¾	1	1	1
Backing	2⅔	3¼	3⅔	3⅔

Directions

Place Fabric A with Fabric B, right sides together, and make the number of large 5" x 5" (4½" x 4½" finished) half-square triangle units required for your quilt size. Use your favorite method or the grid method on page 13. If you use the grid method, draw 3 x 4 grids to make 24 half-square triangle units per grid. Draw grid squares 5⅜" x 5⅜".

Make 32 (#1).
60 (#2).
84 (#3).
96 (#4).

Block 1

1. Sew together 4 Fabric A/B and 4 Fabric A/C cutaway half-square triangle units as shown.

2. Arrange and sew each of these larger units to a large half-square triangle unit as shown.

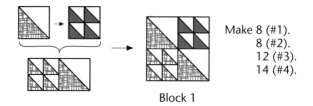

Make 8 (#1).
8 (#2).
12 (#3).
14 (#4).

Block 1

Block 2

1. Sew together 4 Fabric A/B and 4 Fabric B/C cutaway half-square triangle units as shown.

2. Arrange and sew each of these larger units to a large half-square triangle unit, as shown.

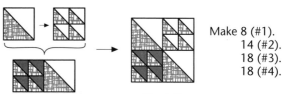

Make 8 (#1).
14 (#2).
18 (#3).
18 (#4).

Block 2

Block 3

1. For Sizes #2, #3, and #4, sew together 4 Fabric A/C and 4 Fabric B/C cutaway half-square triangle units as shown.

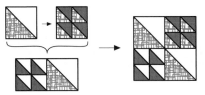

2. Arrange and sew each of these larger units to a large half-square triangle unit, as shown.

Make 8 (#2).
12 (#3).
16 (#4).

Assembling the Quilt Top

1. Arrange blocks according to the quilt plan on page 75 or in any way you prefer. (Make Size #1 using only Blocks 1 and 2.) Sew blocks into rows. Press seam allowances in opposite directions from row to row. Sew rows together. Press.

2. Cut border strips 3½" wide. Refer to the cutting chart for the number of strips for your quilt size. Join strips as needed. Measure, cut, and add side borders as instructed on page 17. Repeat for top and bottom borders.

3½"-wide Border Strips (cut crosswise)				
	#1	#2	#3	#4
No. of Strips	4	6	7	7

3. Layer backing, batting, and quilt top. Quilt as desired and bind the edges. See directions on pages 18–20.

two *without* **ONE**   *To make Flock without first making Hope of Hartford:*

Fabric

In addition to the yardage requirements given in the chart for the Flock quilt on page 76, purchase additional fabric to make 2¾" x 2¾" (2¼" x 2¼" finished) half-square triangle units.

Fabric Requirements in Yards				
	#1	#2	#3	#4
Fabric A	¾	1	1	1½
Fabric B	¾	1	1	1½
Fabric C	¾	1	1	1½

Directions

1. Referring to the cutaways chart for the Flock quilt on page 76, make the number of small half-square triangle units from Fabrics A and B, A and C, and B and C required for the quilt size you are making. Use your favorite method or the grid method on page 13. If you use the grid method, draw 4 x 5 grids to make 40 half-square triangle units per grid. Draw the grid squares 3⅛" x 3⅛".

2. Sew large (4½" finished) half-square triangle units from Fabrics A and B. Assemble blocks, add borders, and complete the quilt. Follow the directions for the Flock quilt, beginning on page 76.

King's X

❑ **Block Size: 15"**
❑ **Color photo: page 28**

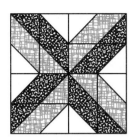

Fabric Key

☐ Fabric A

▨ Fabric B

▨ Fabric C

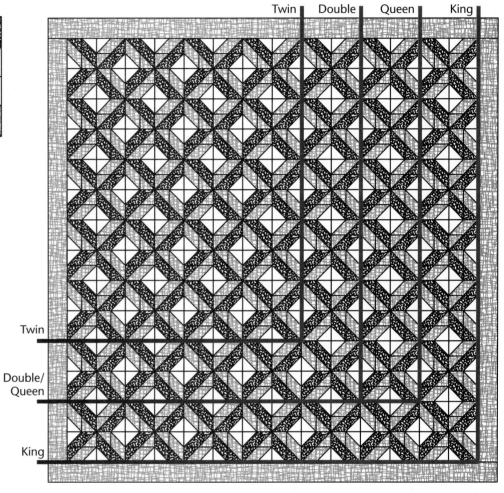

	Twin	Double	Queen	King
Size	70" x 85"	85" x 100"	100" x 100"	115" x 115"
No. of Blocks	20	30	36	49
Set	4 x 5	5 x 6	6 x 6	7 x 7

Fabric

Purchase the required yardage for the quilt size you are making.

Fabric Requirements in Yards

	Twin	Double	Queen	King
Fabric A	2⅓	3¾	4⅛	5¾
Fabric B	3⅜	5¼	6	8
Fabric C	3⅜	5¼	6	8
Border (crosswise)	1⅜	1½	1⅔	2
OR				
Border (lengthwise)	2⅝	2⅞	2⅞	3½
Binding	¾	1	1	1¼
Backing	5⅛	6	9	10⅛

Cutting

Cut all strips across the width of the fabric (crosswise grain).

	First Cut		Second Cut	
	Strip Width	No. of Strips	Dimensions	No. of Pieces
Twin				
Fabric A	4¼"	18	4¼" x 4¼"	160
Fabric B	8"	9	4¼" x 8"	80
	4¼"	9	4¼" x 4¼"	80
Fabric C	8"	9	4¼" x 8"	80
	4¼"	9	4¼" x 4¼"	80
Double				
Fabric A	4¼"	27	4¼" x 4¼"	240
Fabric B	8"	14	4¼" x 8"	120
	4¼"	14	4¼" x 4¼"	120
Fabric C	8"	14	4¼" x 8"	120
	4¼"	14	4¼" x 4¼"	120
Queen				
Fabric A	4¼"	32	4¼" x 4¼"	288
Fabric B	8"	16	4¼" x 8"	144
	4¼"	16	4¼" x 4¼"	144
Fabric C	8"	16	4¼" x 8"	144
	4¼"	16	4¼" x 4¼"	144
King				
Fabric A	4¼"	44	4¼" x 4¼"	392
Fabric B	8"	22	4¼" x 8"	196
	4¼"	22	4¼" x 4¼"	196
Fabric C	8"	22	4¼" x 8"	196
	4¼"	22	4¼" x 4¼"	196

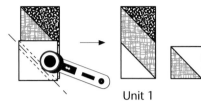

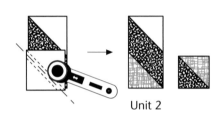

Unit 1

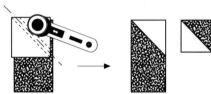

Unit 2

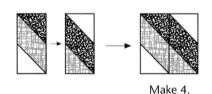

Make 4.

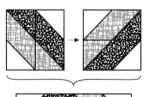

Directions

1. Place a 4¼" square of Fabric B on a 4¼" x 8" rectangle of Fabric C, right sides together. Stitch a diagonal seam, draw a line ½" from the seam, then stitch on this line. Cut between the 2 seams. Press the seam allowances toward Fabric B. Reserve the cutaway half-square triangle unit for the second quilt.

2. Sew a 4¼" square of Fabric A to the opposite end of the rectangle, right sides together, stitching a diagonal seam parallel to the first seam as shown. Stitch a second seam ½" from the first as in step 1. Cut between the 2 seams and press as in step 1. Reserve the cutaway half-square triangle unit.

3. Place a 4¼" square of Fabric A on one end of a 4¼" x 8" rectangle of Fabric B, right sides together. Repeat directions in step 1 above.

4. Sew a 4¼" square of Fabric C to the opposite end of the rectangle, right sides together. Repeat directions in step 2 above to complete Unit 2.

5. Sew Unit 1 to Unit 2 as shown. Make 4 double units for each block.

6. Sew these double units together, rotating each one 90° to make the block as shown.

7. Sew blocks into rows. Press seam allowances in opposite directions from row to row. Sew rows together. Press.

8. Cut border strips 5½" wide. Refer to the cutting chart below for the number of strips for your quilt size. Join strips as needed. Measure, cut, and add side borders as instructed on page 17. Repeat for top and bottom borders.

5½"-wide Border Strips (cut crosswise)

	Twin	Double	Queen	King
No. of Strips	8	9	10	11

9. Layer backing, batting, and quilt top. Quilt as desired and bind the edges. See directions on pages 18–20.

Year's Favorite

❏ **Block Size: 12"**
❏ **Color photo: page 28**

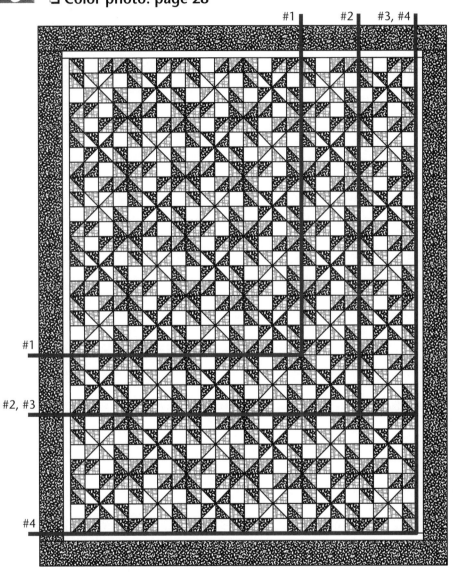

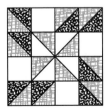

Block 1

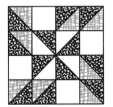

Block 2

Fabric Key

☐ Fabric A

▨ Fabric B

▨ Fabric C

	#1	#2	#3	#4
Size	61" x 73"	73" x 85"	85" x 85"	85" x 109"
No. of Blocks	20	30	36	48
Set	4 x 5	5 x 6	6 x 6	6 x 8

To make Year's Favorite, you will need the following number of 3½" x 3½" (3" x 3" finished) cutaway half-square triangle units. Refer to the second chart for the number of cutaways remaining from each size of King's X. Use extra cutaways for a border or another project.

Total cutaways *needed* for Year's Favorite				
	#1	#2	#3	#4
Fabric A/B	40	60	72	96
Fabric A/C	40	60	72	96
Fabric B/C	160	240	288	384

Cutaways *remaining* from King's X				
	Twin	Double	Queen	King
Fabric A/B	80	120	144	196
Fabric A/C	80	120	144	196
Fabric B/C	160	240	288	392

Note: To use as many of the cutaway half-square triangle units as possible, make an equal number of Blocks 1 and 2. Use remaining units for another quilt project.

Fabric

Purchase additional yardage for the quilt size you are making.

Fabric Requirements in Yards				
	#1	#2	#3	#4
Fabric A	⅞	1¼	1½	2
Inner Border	⅜	½	⅝	⅝
Outer Border (crosswise)	1¼	1⅜	1½	1¾
OR				
Outer Border (lengthwise)	2⅛	2½	2½	3
Binding	¾	1	1	1¼
Backing	3¾	5⅛	7⅝	7⅝

Cutting

Cut all strips across the width of the fabric (crosswise grain). Cut 3½"-wide strips, then cut at 3½" intervals to make squares.

Fabric A				
	#1	#2	#3	#4
Strips	8	11	14	18
Squares	80	120	144	192

Directions

Block 1

Arrange 8 Fabric B/C and 4 Fabric A/C cutaway half-square triangle units with 4 squares of Fabric A, paying careful attention to color placement. Make the number of blocks required for your quilt size.

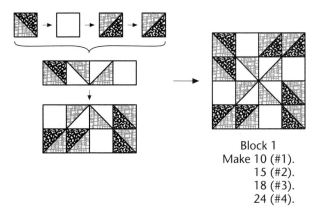

Block 1
Make 10 (#1).
15 (#2).
18 (#3).
24 (#4).

Block 2

Arrange 8 Fabric B/C and 4 Fabric A/B cutaway half-square triangle units with 4 squares of Fabric A, paying careful attention to color placement. Make the number of blocks required for your quilt size.

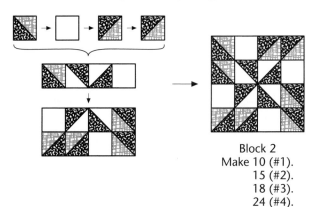

Block 2
Make 10 (#1).
15 (#2).
18 (#3).
24 (#4).

Assembling the Quilt Top

1. Alternating Blocks 1 and 2, arrange and sew blocks together into rows. Press seam allowances in opposite directions from row to row. Sew rows together. Press.

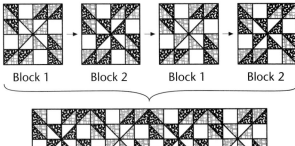

Block 1 → Block 2 → Block 1 → Block 2

Block 2 Block 1 Block 2 Block 1

2. Cut inner border strips 2" wide. Refer to the cutting chart below for the number of strips for your quilt size. Join strips as needed. Measure, cut, and add side borders as instructed on page 17. Repeat for top and bottom borders.

Border Strips (cut crosswise)

Strip Width	No. of Strips			
	#1	#2	#3	#4
2"	6	7	8	9
5½"	7	8	9	10

3. Repeat step 2 for outer border, cutting strips 5½" wide and joining strips as needed.

4. Layer backing, batting, and quilt top. Quilt as desired and bind the edges. See directions on pages 18–20.

two without ONE

To make Year's Favorite without first making King's X:

Fabric

In addition to the yardage requirements given in the chart on page 82 for the Year's Favorite quilt, purchase fabric to make 3½" x 3½" (3" x 3" finished) half-square triangle units.

Fabric Requirements in Yards

	#1	#2	#3	#4
Fabric A	½	1	1	1½
Fabric B	1½	2	2⅜	2⅞
Fabric C	1½	2	2⅜	2⅞

Directions

1. Referring to the chart for cutaways on page 82, make the number of half-square triangle units for your quilt size, combining pieces of Fabrics A and B, A and C, and B and C. Use your favorite method or the grid method on page 13. If you use the grid method, draw 4 x 5 grids to make 40 half-square triangles each. Draw grid squares 3⅞" x 3⅞".

2. Referring to the cutting chart on page 82, cut the required number of Fabric A squares needed for your quilt size.

3. Assemble blocks, add borders, and finish the quilt, following the directions for the Year's Favorite quilt, beginning on page 82.

ONE Arkansas Traveler

❏ **Block Size: 15"**
❏ **Color photo: page 35**

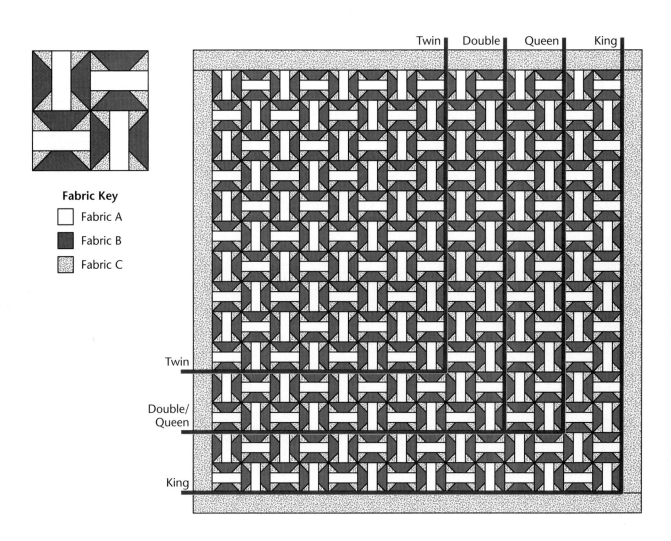

Fabric Key

☐ Fabric A
■ Fabric B
▨ Fabric C

	Twin	Double	Queen	King
Size	70" x 85"	85" x 100"	100" x 100"	115" x 115"
No. of Blocks	20	30	36	49
Set	4 x 5	5 x 6	6 x 6	7 x 7

Fabric

Purchase the required yardage for the quilt size you are making.

Fabric Requirements in Yards

	Twin	Double	Queen	King
Fabric A	1⅞	2½	3	3⅞
Fabric B	3¼*	4⅝	5⅜**	7⅜
Fabric C	2⅜*	3⅜	4⅛**	5⅜
Border (crosswise)	1⅜	1½	1¾	2
OR				
Border (lengthwise)	2⅝	2⅞	2⅞	3⅜
Binding	¾	1	1	1¼
Backing	5¼	6	9	10⅛

*If you make Arkansas Traveler in the Twin size and want to make Hovering Hawks secondary quilt in Size #1, increase yardage to 3⅝ yards of Fabric B and 2⅞ yards of Fabric C.

**If you make Arkansas Traveler in the Queen size and want to make Hovering Hawks in Size #2, increase yardage to 6⅛ yards of Fabric B and 4¾ yards of Fabric C.

Cutting

Cut all strips across the width of the fabric (crosswise grain).

	First Cut		**Second Cut**	
	Strip Width	No. of Strips	Dimensions	No. of Pieces
Twin				
Fabric A	8"	7	3" x 8"	80
Fabric B	8"	13	3" x 8"	160
Fabric C	3"	25	3" x 3"	320
Double				
Fabric A	8"	10	3" x 8"	120
Fabric B	8"	19	3" x 8"	240
Fabric C	3"	37	3" x 3"	480
Queen				
Fabric A	8"	12	3" x 8"	144
Fabric B	8"	23	3" x 8"	288
Fabric C	3"	45	3" x 3"	576
King				
Fabric A	8"	16	3" x 8"	196
Fabric B	8"	31	3" x 8"	392
Fabric C	3"	61	3" x 3"	784

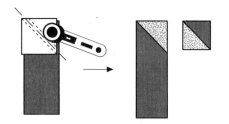

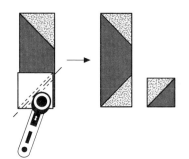

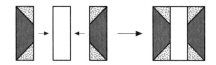

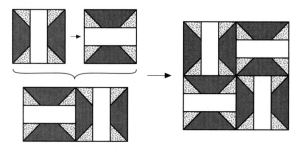

Directions

1. Place a 3" square of Fabric C on a 3" x 8" rectangle of Fabric B, right sides together. Sew a diagonal seam, draw a line ½" from the seam, then sew on this line. Cut between the 2 seams. Reserve the cutaway half-square triangle unit for the second quilt.

2. Place a second square of Fabric C on the opposite end of the rectangle and sew a diagonal seam perpendicular to the first seam as shown. Sew a second seam ½" from the first; cut between the seams. Reserve the cutaway half-square triangle unit.

Note: Press the seam allowances toward Fabric C. You can save time if you sew both squares to the rectangle before you press.

3. Sew a unit from step 2 to each side of a 3" x 8" rectangle of Fabric A as shown.

4. Sew 4 of these larger units together, rotating each 90° to make the block as shown.

5. Referring to the quilt diagram on page 84, arrange and sew the blocks into rows. Press seam allowances in opposite directions from row to row. Sew rows together. Press.

6. Cut border strips 5½" wide. Refer to the cutting chart below for the number of strips for your quilt size. Join strips as needed. Measure, cut, and add side borders as instructed on page 17. Repeat for top and bottom borders.

5½"-wide Border Strips (cut crosswise)

	Twin	Double	Queen	King
No. of Strips	8	9	10	12

7. Layer backing, batting, and quilt top. Quilt as desired and bind the edges. See directions on pages 18–20.

Hovering Hawks

❏ **Block Size: 7"**
❏ **Color photo: page 35**

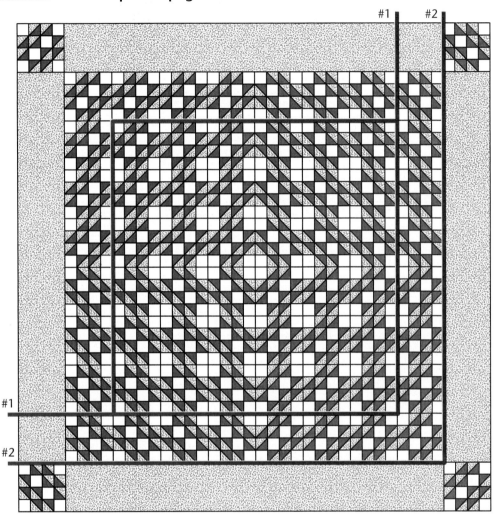

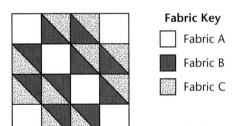

Fabric Key

☐ Fabric A

■ Fabric B

▨ Fabric C

Note: If you make Arkansas Traveler in the Twin size and want to make Size #1, construct 80 additional half-square triangle units from Fabrics B and C. If you make Arkansas Traveler in the Queen size and want to make Size #2, construct 104 additional half-square triangle units from Fabrics B and C. (For yardage requirements, see Fabric chart on page 88.) Use your favorite method or the grid method on page 13. If you use the grid method, draw 4 x 5 grids to make 40 half-square triangle units each. Draw grid squares 2⅝" x 2⅝".

	#1	#2
Size	56" x 56"	70" x 70"
No. of Blocks	40*	68*
Set	6 x 6	8 x 8

Reserve 4 blocks for border.

To make Hovering Hawks, you will need the following number of 2¼" x 2¼" (1¾" x 1¾" finished) cutaway half-square triangle units. Refer to the second chart for the number of cutaways remaining from each size of Arkansas Traveler. Use extra cutaways for a border or another project.

Total cutaways *needed* for Hovering Hawks

	#1	#2
Fabric B/C	400	680

Cutaways *remaining* from Arkansas Traveler

	Twin	Double	Queen	King
Fabric B/C	320	480	576	784

Fabric

Purchase additional fabric required for the quilt size you are making.

Fabric Requirements in Yards

	#1	#2
Fabric A	1⅛	1¾
Border (crosswise)	1¼	1¾
OR		
Border (lengthwise)	1⅔	2⅛
Binding	¾	1
Backing	3½	4¼

Cutting

Cut 2¼"-wide strips, then cut at 2¼" intervals to make 2¼" squares.

Size	#1		#2	
	Strips	Squares	Strips	Squares
Fabric A	15	240	24	408

Directions

1. For each block, you will need 10 cutaway half-square triangle units and 6 squares of Fabric A, measuring 2¼" x 2¼". Arrange and sew squares and half-square triangle units into blocks.

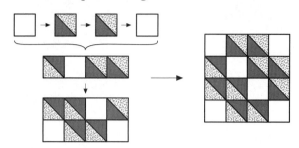

2. Arrange the blocks, following the quilt plan on page 87 for the size you are making. Be sure to place pieced blocks with the fabrics and seams oriented in the direction shown in the quilt plan. Reserve 4 blocks for corners.

3. Sew blocks into rows. Press seam allowances in opposite directions from row to row. Sew rows together. Press.

4. Cut border strips 7½" wide. Refer to the cutting chart below for the number of strips for your quilt size. Join strips as needed. Measure through the center of the quilt and cut all 4 borders to this measurement. Add side borders as instructed on page 17. Press.

7½"-wide Border Strips (cut crosswise)

	#1	#2
No. of Strips	5	6

5. Sew a Hovering Hawks block to each end of the top and bottom borders, paying careful attention to the orientation of fabrics and seams. Sew top and bottom borders to quilt. Press.

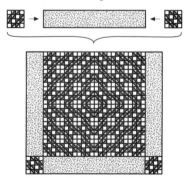

6. Layer backing, batting, and quilt top. Quilt as desired and bind the edges. See directions on pages 18–20.

To make Hovering Hawks without first making Arkansas Traveler:

Fabric

In addition to the yardage requirements given in the chart on page 88 for the Hovering Hawks quilt, purchase fabric to make 2¼" x 2¼" (1¾" x 1¾" finished) half-square triangle units.

Fabric Requirements in Yards

	#1	#2
Fabric B	1¼	2½
Fabric C	1¼	2½

Directions

1. Combine pieces of Fabrics B and C to make the number of 2¼" x 2¼" half-square triangle units required for your quilt size. (Refer to the chart for cutaways on page 88 for numbers of units needed.) Use your favorite method or the grid method on page 13. If you use the grid method, draw 5 x 7 grids to make 70 half-square triangle units each. Draw grid squares 2⅝" x 2⅝".

2. Cut 2¼" squares of Fabric A and combine them with half-square triangle units to assemble blocks. Add borders and finish the quilt, following steps 1–6 on page 88 for the Hovering Hawks quilt.

ONE Aerial Spelunker

❑ **Block Size: 16"**
❑ **Color photo: page 30**

Fabric Key

☐ Fabric A

▨ Fabric B

▧ Fabric C

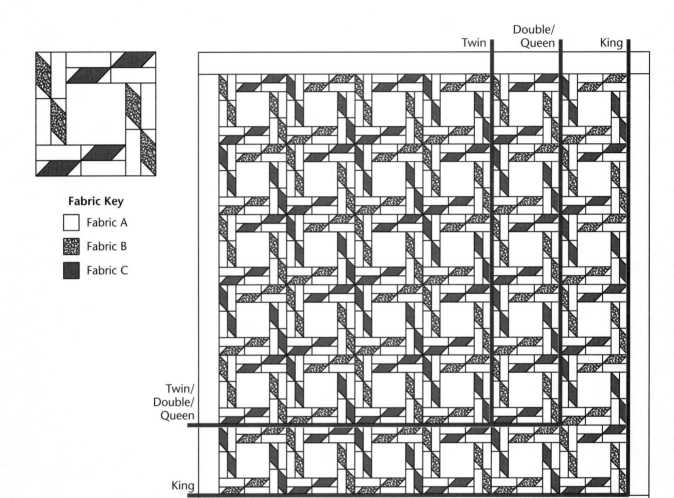

	Twin	Double/Queen	King
Size	74" x 90"	90" x 90"	106" x 106"
No. of Blocks	20	25	36
Set	4 x 5	5 x 5	6 x 6

Fabric

Purchase the required yardage for the quilt size you are making.

Fabric Requirements in Yards

	Twin	Double/Queen	King
Fabric A	$4\frac{5}{8}$	6	$8\frac{1}{4}$
Fabric B	$1\frac{1}{8}$	$1\frac{1}{2}$	$1\frac{7}{8}$
Fabric C	$1\frac{1}{8}$	$1\frac{1}{2}$	$1\frac{7}{8}$
Border (crosswise)	$1\frac{3}{8}$	$1\frac{1}{2}$	$1\frac{7}{8}$
OR			
Border (lengthwise)	$2\frac{5}{8}$	$2\frac{5}{8}$	$3\frac{1}{8}$
Binding	$\frac{3}{4}$	1	$1\frac{1}{4}$
Backing	$5\frac{1}{3}$	8	$9\frac{1}{3}$

Cutting

Cut all strips across the width of the fabric (crosswise grain).

	First Cut		Second Cut	
	Strip Width	No. of Strips	Dimensions	No. of Pieces
Twin				
Fabric A	$8\frac{1}{2}$"	5	$8\frac{1}{2}$" x $8\frac{1}{2}$"	20
	$6\frac{1}{2}$"	10	$2\frac{1}{2}$" x $6\frac{1}{2}$"	160
	$2\frac{1}{2}$"	20	$2\frac{1}{2}$" x $2\frac{1}{2}$"	320
Fabric B	$6\frac{1}{2}$"	5	$2\frac{1}{2}$" x $6\frac{1}{2}$"	80
Fabric C	$6\frac{1}{2}$"	5	$2\frac{1}{2}$" x $6\frac{1}{2}$"	80
Double/Queen				
Fabric A	$8\frac{1}{2}$"	7	$8\frac{1}{2}$" x $8\frac{1}{2}$"	25
	$6\frac{1}{2}$"	13	$2\frac{1}{2}$" x $6\frac{1}{2}$"	200
	$2\frac{1}{2}$"	25	$2\frac{1}{2}$" x $2\frac{1}{2}$"	400
Fabric B	$6\frac{1}{2}$"	7	$2\frac{1}{2}$" x $6\frac{1}{2}$"	100
Fabric C	$6\frac{1}{2}$"	7	$2\frac{1}{2}$" x $6\frac{1}{2}$"	100
King				
Fabric A	$8\frac{1}{2}$"	9	$8\frac{1}{2}$"x $8\frac{1}{2}$"	36
	$6\frac{1}{2}$"	18	$2\frac{1}{2}$" x $6\frac{1}{2}$"	288
	$2\frac{1}{2}$"	36	$2\frac{1}{2}$" x $2\frac{1}{2}$"	576
Fabric B	$6\frac{1}{2}$"	9	$2\frac{1}{2}$" x $6\frac{1}{2}$"	144
Fabric C	$6\frac{1}{2}$"	9	$2\frac{1}{2}$" x $6\frac{1}{2}$"	144

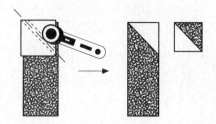

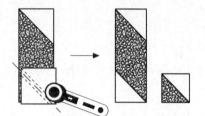

Directions

1. Place a 2½" Fabric A square on a 2½" x 6" Fabric B rectangle, right sides together. Sew a diagonal seam, draw a line ½" from the seam, then sew on this line. Cut between the 2 seams. Press the seam allowances toward the Fabric A triangle. Reserve the cutaway half-square triangle unit for the second quilt.

2. Sew a 2½" Fabric A square to the opposite end of the rectangle, sewing a diagonal seam parallel to the first seam as shown. Sew a second seam ½" from the first. Cut between the 2 seams and press the seam allowances toward the Fabric A triangle. Reserve the cutaway half-square triangle unit.

3. Following the directions in steps 1 and 2, sew a Fabric A square to each end of a 2½" x 6" Fabric C rectangle. Reserve the cutaway half-square triangle units.

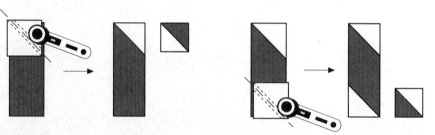

4. Sew a 2½" x 6½" Fabric A rectangle to each of the units as shown.

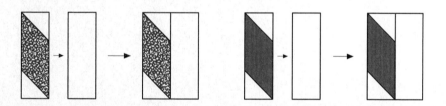

5. Sew 2 Fabric A/B units together and 2 Fabric A/C units together as shown. Make 2 sets of each fabric combination for each block.

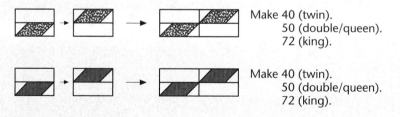

Make 40 (twin).
50 (double/queen).
72 (king).

Make 40 (twin).
50 (double/queen).
72 (king).

6. Place a Fabric A/B unit right sides together with an 8½" Fabric A square. Sew a half-seam as shown. It will be completed later.

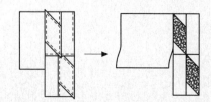

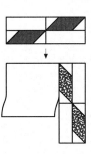

7. Sew a Fabric A/C unit to the side, sewing a complete seam as shown.

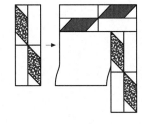

8. Sew a Fabric A/B unit to the third side of the block as shown.

9. Sew a Fabric A/C unit to the fourth side of the block as shown.

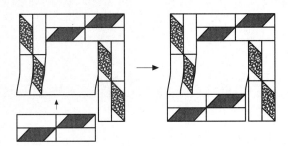

10. Complete the first seam.

11. Arrange the blocks, rotating alternating blocks 90° as shown in the quilt plan on page 90. Sew blocks into rows. Press seam allowances in opposite directions from row to row. Sew rows together. Press.

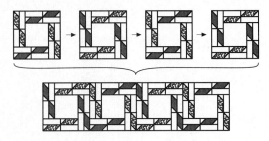

12. Cut border strips 5½" wide. Refer to the cutting chart below for the number of strips for your quilt size. Join strips as needed. Measure, cut, and add side borders as instructed on page 17. Repeat for top and bottom borders.

5½"-wide Border Strips (cut crosswise)

	Twin	Double/Queen	King
Number of Strips	8	9	11

13. Layer backing, batting, and quilt top. Quilt as desired and bind the edges. See directions on pages 18–20.

two Indian Trails

- ❏ **Block Size: 10"**
- ❏ **Color photo: page 30**

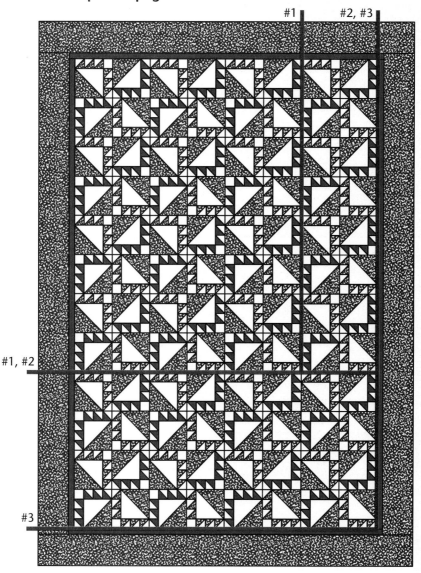

Fabric Key

- ☐ Fabric A
- ▨ Fabric B
- ▦ Fabric C

	#1	**#2**	**#3**
Size	40" x 50"	50" x 50"	50" x 70"
No. of Blocks	12	16	24
Set	3 x 4	4 x 4	4 x 6

To make Indian Trails, you will need the following number of 1¾" x 1¾" (1¼" x 1¼" finished) cutaway half-square triangle units. Refer to the second chart for the number of cutaways remaining from each size of Aerial Spelunker. Use extra cutaways for a border or another project.

Total cutaways *needed* for Indian Trails

	#1	#2	#3
Fabrics A/B	144	192	288
Fabrics A/C	144	192	288

Cutaways *remaining* from Aerial Spelunker

	Twin	Double/Queen	King
Fabrics A/B	160	200	288
Fabrics A/C	160	200	288

Fabric

Purchase additional fabric for your quilt size to make 4¼" x 4¼" (3¾" x 3¾" finished) large half-square triangle units and 1¾" x 1¾" background squares.

Fabric Requirements in Yards

	#1	#2	#3
Fabric A	⅞	1⅝	1¾
Fabric B	⅔	1⅜	1⅜
Inner Border (crosswise)	¼	¼	⅓
Outer Border (lengthwise)	¾	¾	⅞
Binding	½	¾	¾
Backing	1⅝	3¼	3¼

Cutting

Cut all strips across the width of the fabric (crosswise grain). Cut 1¾"-wide strips, then cut at 1¾" intervals to make squares.

Fabric A

	#1	#2	#3
Strips	3	3	5
Squares	48	64	96

Directions

1. Place the large, uncut piece of Fabric A on Fabric B, right sides together. Using either your favorite method or the grid method on page 13, make the number of large 4¼" x 4¼" (3¼" x 3¼" finished) half-square triangle units required for your quilt size. If you use the grid method, draw 3 x 4 grids to make 24 half-square triangle units per grid. Draw grid squares 4⅝" x 4⅝".

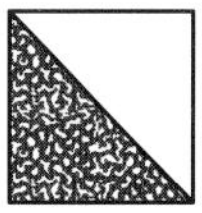

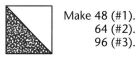

Make 48 (#1).
64 (#2).
96 (#3).

2. Sew together 3 small Fabric A/B cutaway half-square triangle units to form Unit 1, paying careful attention to dark and light fabric placement as shown.

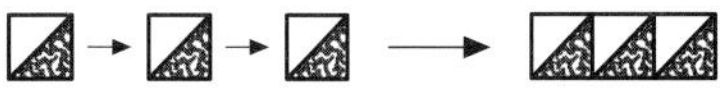

Unit 1

Make 24 (#1).
32 (#2).
48 (#3).

3. Sew Unit 1 to a large half-square triangle as shown to make Unit 2.

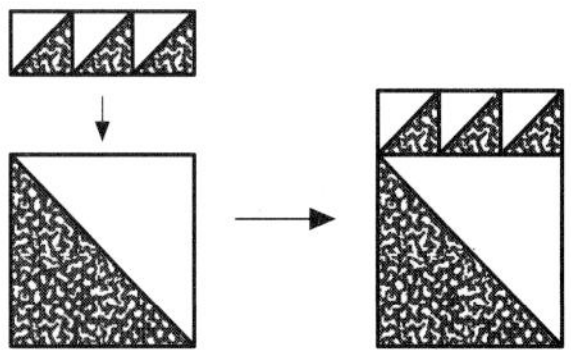

Unit 2

4. Sew together 3 more small Fabric A/B cutaway half-square triangle units, noting placement. Sew a 1¾" Fabric A square to one end to make Unit 3 as shown.

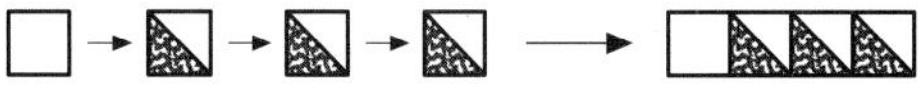

Unit 3

Make 24 (#1).
32 (#2).
48 (#3).

5. Sew Unit 2 to Unit 3 as shown.

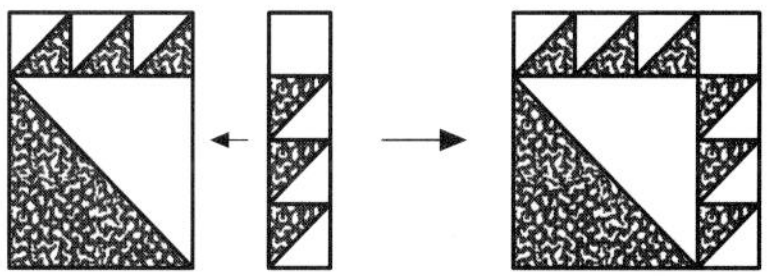

6. Repeat steps 1–4, using small Fabric A/C half-square triangle units in place of small Fabric A/B half-square triangle units.

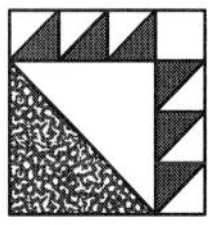

7. Arrange and sew 2 A/B units and 2 A/C units to make the block, alternating units and turning each 90° as shown.

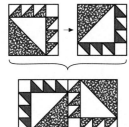

8. Sew blocks into rows. Press seam allowances in opposite directions from row to row. Sew rows together. Press.

9. Cut inner border strips 1¼" wide. Refer to the cutting chart above right for the number of strips for your quilt size. Join strips as needed. Measure, cut, and add side borders as directed on page 17. Repeat for top and bottom borders.

Border Strips (cut crosswise)

Strip Width	No. of Strips		
	#1	#2	#3
1¼"	4	5	6
4¼"	5	5	6

10. Repeat step 9 for outer border, cutting strips 4½" wide and joining strips as needed.

11. Layer backing, batting, and quilt top. Quilt as desired and bind the edges. See directions on pages 18–20.

To make Indian Trails without first making Aerial Spelunker:

Fabric

In addition to the yardage requirements given in the chart on page 94 for the Indian Trails quilt, purchase fabric to make 1¾" x 1¾" (1¼" x 1¼" finished) half-square triangle units.

Note: for half-square triangle units this small, I recommend using the bias-strip method on pages 14–15 for making multiple half-square triangle units. Follow the directions in the cutting chart at right to make 13½" x 42" or 13½" x 22" pieces.

Fabric Requirements in Yards

	#1	#2	#3
Fabric A	1	1¼	1⅔
Fabric B	½	⅞	⅞
Fabric C	½	⅞	⅞

Cutting

Number of Pieces

	#1	#2	#3
Fabric A			
13½" x 42" Pieces	2	2	4
13½" x 22" Pieces		2	
Fabric B			
13½" x 42" Pieces	1	1	2
13½" x 22" Pieces		1	
Fabric C			
13½" x 42" Pieces	1	1	2
13½" x 22" Pieces		1	

Directions

1. Combine Fabrics A and B and Fabrics B and C to make the number of 1¾" x 1¾" half-square triangle units for your quilt size.

    Make 144 each (#1).
192 each (#2).
288 each (#3).

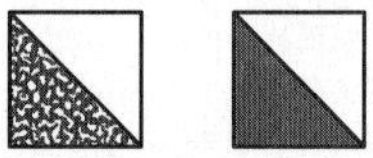

2. Assemble blocks, add borders, and finish the quilt. Follow steps 1–11, beginning on page 95, for the Indian Trails quilt.

Ribbons

❏ **Block Size: 15"**
❏ **Color photo: page 32**

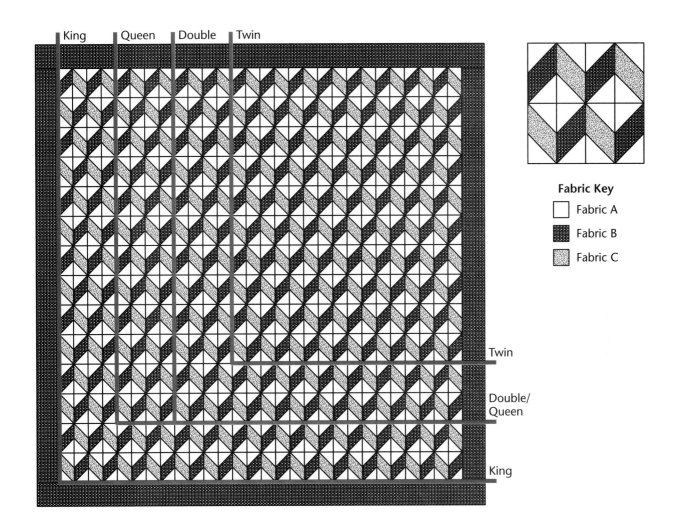

Fabric Key

☐ Fabric A
▨ Fabric B
▨ Fabric C

	Twin	Double	Queen	King
Size	72" x 87"	87" x 102"	102" x 102"	117" x 117"
No. of Blocks	20	30	36	49
Set	4 x 5	5 x 6	6 x 6	7 x 7

Fabric

Purchase the required yardage for the quilt size you are making.

Fabric Requirements in Yards

	Twin	Double	Queen	King
Fabric A	4½	6⅞	8	10⅞
Fabric B	2¼	3½	4	5⅜
Fabric C	2¼	3½	4	5⅜
Border (crosswise)	1⅝	1⅞	2	2⅜
OR				
Border (lengthwise)	2½	3	3	3⅜
Binding	¾	1	1	1¼
Backing	5	8½	9	10¾

Cutting

Cut all strips across the width of the fabric (crosswise grain).

	First Cut		Second Cut	
	Strip Width	No. of Strips	Dimensions	No. of Pieces
Twin				
Fabric A	4¼"	36	4¼" x 4¼"	320
Fabric B	8"	9	4¼" x 8"	80
Fabric C	8"	9	4¼" x 8"	80
Double				
Fabric A	4¼"	54	4¼" x 4¼"	480
Fabric B	8"	14	4¼" x 8"	120
Fabric C	8"	14	4¼" x 8"	120
Queen				
Fabric A	4¼"	64	4¼" x 4¼"	576
Fabric B	8"	16	4¼" x 8"	144
Fabric C	8"	16	4¼" x 8"	144
King				
Fabric A	4¼"	88	4¼" x 4¼"	784
Fabric B	8"	22	4¼" x 8"	196
Fabric C	8"	22	4¼" x 8"	196

Directions

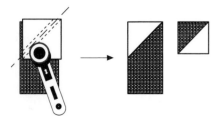

1. To make unit 1, place a 4¼" square of Fabric A on a 4¼" x 8" rectangle of Fabric B, right sides together. Sew a diagonal seam from the upper right corner as shown. Draw a line ½" from the seam, then sew on this line. Cut between the 2 seams. Press seam allowances toward the Fabric A triangle. Reserve the cutaway half-square triangle unit for the second quilt.

2. Sew a 4¼" square of Fabric A to the opposite end of the rectangle, sewing a diagonal seam parallel to the first seam as shown. Sew a second seam ½" from the first. Cut between the 2 seams and press the seam allowances toward Fabric A. Reserve the cutaway half-square triangle unit.

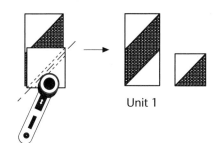

Unit 1

3. To make unit 2, repeat steps 1 and 2 with a 4¼" x 8" rectangle of Fabric C and 4¼" squares of Fabric A. Sew the diagonal seam from the upper left corner of the square as shown.

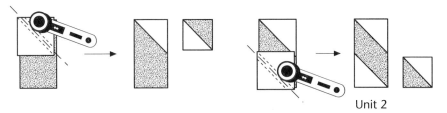

Unit 2

4. Sew a Unit 1 to each Unit 2 as shown.

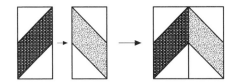

5. Sew 4 large units from step 4 together to make the block, rotating the second units 180° as shown. Make the required number of blocks for your quilt size.

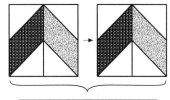

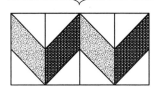

6. Sew blocks into rows. Press seam allowances in opposite directions from row to row. Sew rows together. Press.

7. Cut border strips 6½" wide. Refer to the cutting chart below for the number of strips for your quilt size. Join strips as needed. Measure, cut, and add side borders as directed on page 17. Repeat for top and bottom borders.

6½"-wide Border Strips (cut crosswise)

	Twin	Double	Queen	King
No. of Strips	8	9	10	12

8. Layer backing, batting, and quilt top. Quilt as desired and bind the edges. See directions on pages 18–20.

Dutchman's Puzzle

❑ **Block Size:** 12"
❑ **Color photo:** page 32

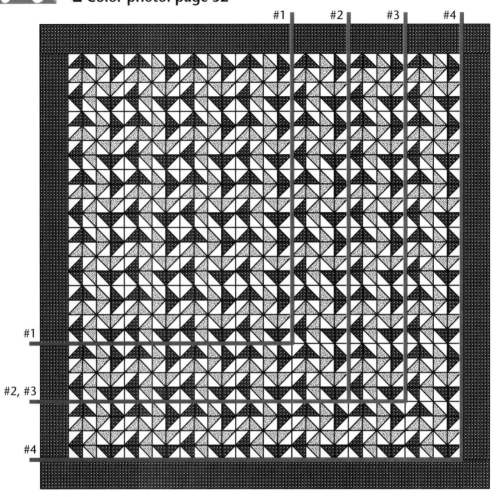

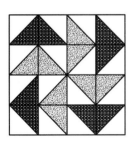

Fabric Key

☐ Fabric A

▨ Fabric B

▨ Fabric C

	#1	#2	#3	#4
Size	60" x 72"	72" x 84"	84" x 84"	96" x 96"
No. of Blocks	20	30	36	49
Set	4 x 5	5 x 6	6 x 6	7 x 7

To make Dutchman's Puzzle, you will need the following number of 3½" x 3½" (3" x 3" finished) cutaway half-square triangle units. Refer to the second chart for the number of cutaways remaining from each size of Ribbons. Use extra cutaways for a border or another project.

Total cutaways *needed* for Dutchman's Puzzle

	#1	#2	#3	#4
Fabric A/B	160	240	288	392
Fabric A/C	160	240	288	392

Cutaways *remaining* from Ribbons

	Twin	Double	Queen	King
Fabrics A/B	160	240	288	392
Fabrics A/C	160	240	288	392

Fabric

Purchase additional fabric for the quilt size you are making.

Fabric Requirements in Yards

	#1	#2	#3	#4
Border (crosswise)	1½	1⅝	1⅝	2
OR				
Border (lengthwise)	2⅛	2½	2½	2¾
Binding	¾	1	1	1¼
Backing	3⅔	4⅓	7½	8½

Directions

1. Sew 2 Fabric A/B cutaway half-square triangle units together to make Unit 1 as shown.

Unit 1

2. Sew 2 Fabric A/C cutaway half-square triangle units together to make Unit 2 as shown.

Unit 2

3. Sew each Unit 1 to a Unit 2 as shown.

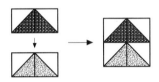

4. Sew 4 of the units from step 2 together to make a block, rotating each unit 90° as shown. Make the required number of blocks for the quilt size you are making.

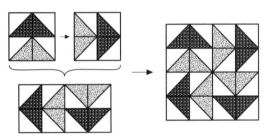

5. Sew blocks into rows. Press seam allowances in opposite directions from row to row. Sew rows together. Press.

6. Cut border strips 6½" wide. Refer to the cutting chart below for the number of strips for your quilt size. Join strips as needed. Measure, cut, and add side borders as directed on page 17. Repeat for top and bottom borders.

6½"-wide Border Strips (cut crosswise)

	#1	#2	#3	#4
No. of Border Strips	7	8	8	10

7. Layer backing, batting, and quilt top. Quilt as desired and bind the edges. See directions on pages 18–20.

To make Dutchman's Puzzle without first making Ribbons:

Fabric

In addition to the yardage requirements given in the chart on page 101 for the Dutchman's Puzzle quilt, purchase fabric to make 3½" x 3½" (3" x 3" finished) half-square triangle units.

Fabric Requirements in Yards				
	#1	#2	#3	#4
Fabric A	2½	3½	4¾	6
Fabric B	1¼	1¾	2½	3
Fabric C	1¼	1¾	2½	3

Directions

1. Combine pieces of Fabrics A and B and pieces of Fabrics A and C to make the number of half-square triangle units for your quilt size. Use your favorite method or the grid method on page 13. For the grid method, draw grids 4 x 5 to make 40 half-square triangle units per grid. Draw grid squares 3⅞" x 3⅞".

2. Assemble blocks, add borders, and finish the quilt, following steps 1–7 on page 101 for the Dutchman's Puzzle quilt.

A Little Extra

After looking at all the quilts and following the procedures included in this book, you can quickly see that many quilts, and borders too, can be made using the "Two for Your Money" idea. On these two pages, you'll find blocks that are suitable for first quilts. Use one of these or one of your own designs, refer to the "Technique" section on pages 6–9, and make a quilt of your choice.

Bow Border

A Little Extra

The following blocks are just a few of the additional blocks that can be made with the cutaway half-square triangle units left over from a first quilt. So much can be done with the squares—just let your mind go—but whatever you do, don't let the squares go to waste. Make something!

Double Hourglass

T (T x T)

Maple Leaf

Broken Dishes

Ladies' Wreath

Sailboat

Hopscotch

Pine Tree

Basket

Tit for Tat

Tall Pine Tree

Bear's Paw

Crow's Foot

Winged Square

Ribbon

Jo Parrott

Jo Parrott was born and raised in the San Joaquin Valley of California, where her parents grew cotton and grapes. She and her husband, Henry, have been together for 32 years and have a "yours, mine, and ours" family of seven children and 16 grandchildren. In 1983, after 25 years of accounting in the automobile industry, Jo left to teach quilting classes and open her own quilt shop. She has written two other books for That Patchwork Place: *Not Just Quilts* and *Template-Free® Stars*.